Praise

"Many professionals reach a point where they've checked all the right boxes, but still feel disconnected from their work. *Seen Known Valued* offers a powerful invitation to rethink what success looks like—not through the lens of roles and resumes, but through the deeper work of aligning your identity with your career. If you're ready to stop shape-shifting for others and start designing a path that reflects your true self, this book is a must-read."

—Dorie Clark, *Wall Street Journal* bestselling Author of *The Long Game* and *Reinventing You*

"In a world in constant flux, *Seen Known Valued* is an invaluable grounding force. Dr. Bickerton beautifully reframes how we navigate our work lives—not by chasing fit or others' ideas for what we "should" do with our careers, but by owning our agency and seeking our own versions of belonging. It's our best shot at bringing our best selves to the world."

—April Rinne, Author of *FLUX: 8 Superpowers for Thriving in Constant Change*

"Seen Known Valued challenges conventional career development. Sarabeth invites readers to rethink how they show up at work—not by conforming and fitting in, but by reclaiming the power of their unique contributions so that we cultivate workplaces where people—and potential—can truly thrive."
—**Julie Winkle Giulioni, Author of Promotions Are So Yesterday and Help Them Grow or Watch Them Go**

"This book is the missing piece in the future of work conversation. Dr. Bickerton shifts the focus from external achievement to internal alignment—and shows us what it really means to feel seen, known, and valued in our careers. It's a profound and practical articulation of what success-FULL can look like for every one of us."
—**Shelley Paxton, Former CMO of Harley-Davidson, now Chief Soul Officer, keynote speaker, and bestselling author of Soulbbatical: A Corporate Rebel's Guide for Finding Your Best Life**

SEEN KNOWN VALUED

HOW TO ACHIEVE CAREER BELONGING IN A WORKFORCE OBSESSED WITH FIT

SARABETH BERK BICKERTON, PHD.

Seen Known Valued: How to Achieve Career Belonging in a Workforce Obsessed with Fit

Ordering Information:
Quantity sales. Special discounts are available on quantity purchases by corporations, associations, and others.

For Brad, Theo, Fudge, Bev, and Phil who
taught me the true meaning of belonging.

Your career is not given to you.

Your career is not decided by anyone

Your career is not predetermined

Your career is not set in stone

Your career is not a path

Your career is not located on a map

Your career is not following in the footsteps of others

Your career is not something you only choose once in your life

Your career is not permanent

Your career is not too messy

Your career is not a set of qualifications to meet

Your career is not over unless you say it is

Your career is whatever you say it is

Your career is up to you

Your career is how you want to be seen

Your career is how you want to be known

Your career is how you want to be valued

Your career belongs to you

It's your life's work

So how will you define your career belonging?

—Dr. Sarabeth Berk Bickerton

Belonging has meant a deep love,
an embrace,
a home,
a space I can come back to,
where I am seen,
where I can laugh,
cry,
be at ease,
in all the many ways I can be.
I find belonging in stories that weave together
generations, with all our messiness and imperfections.
Belonging is unique in different spaces and contexts,
it can be in the arms of a loved one, or in a bowl of a
lovingly cooked meal.

—A'Ishah Wajeed

seenknownvalued.com

Career Belonging Beyond This Book

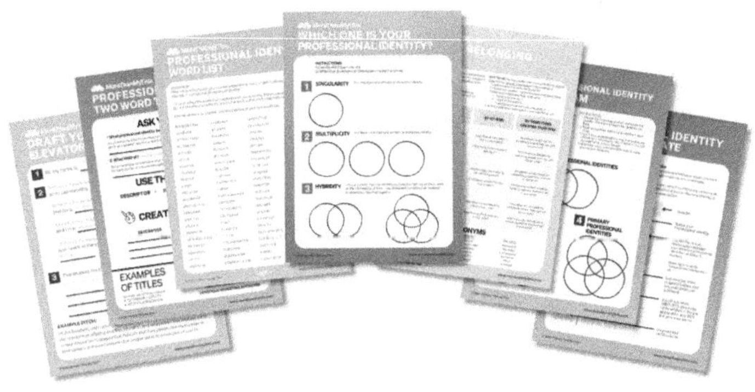

When you're ready to dive deeper, visit my growing library of tools and resources to help you define your professional identity and career belonging.

These materials will aid you in bringing ideas in this book to life so you can readily apply them to your work and career.

Visit the website to find:

- Guided exercises and handouts
- Professional identity development tools
- The AI Companion to this book
- More information about courses and other learning experiences

Contents

Rethinking Modern Careers

We've been told to "find where we fit." The collective narrative is that if we put our skills, talents, qualifications, and economically viable interests together, we'll find a role that brings fulfillment. Yet millions of professionals—especially jacks-of-all-trades—continue to feel unseen, undervalued, and disconnected in their work even when they find their fit.

Why is that?

The career fit industry is doing exactly what it was designed to do: matching people to roles and occupations. And, it's extremely good at this. There's nothing broken about how it works. What is broken is our assumption that fit will bring us acceptance, connection, recognition, and meaning. Fit's purpose is to place people into defined roles, it does not honor the complexity of who we are.

The modern workforce desires something old systems cannot provide.

If we want careers that bring us joy in the morning, a sense of inner peace at day's end, and a deeper connection to something larger than tasks or titles, then we need a new paradigm.

Here's my proposal:

What if we stopped searching for career fit and started aiming for career belonging instead?

Consider this:

What if the core issues keeping us from thriving in our careers stem from the outdated language we use, the conformity we've inherited, and the systems that no longer meet the needs of today's multifaceted professionals?

To understand this, let me introduce you to Sue.

Sue's Desire? To Find Her "Place"

Sue recently made the difficult decision to leave her job, driven by a desire to find a place where she truly belonged. "I'm not looking for a career in the traditional sense," she told me over coffee. "I don't need it, I don't want it. I feel blessed that I can make this decision. The hard part is figuring out what to do with my time and what to call it. For now, it's about finding something that brings me joy, gets me out of bed, and allows me to help people."

Sue was in her early fifties, with a respected career behind her. But despite her achievements, something inside her had been eroding for years. Internal politics, shifting alliances, and unspoken bias slowly undermined her confidence and contributions. She kept waiting for things to improve—after the next project, after the next restructuring, after the boss retired—but they never did. These dynamics left her feeling minimized and undervalued, unable to fully show up and contribute as she once had.

Eventually, her inner voice grew louder and nudged her towards something different. Sue knew she was done trying to fit in. During the COVID lockdown, she did an exercise that asked her to identify a single word that captured her essence. With a warm smile spreading across her face, she said it to me: *"Place."*

Place represented something Sue never knew she was missing: not a role, not a title, but somewhere she could feel at home in her work and be herself.

In academic literature, place and belonging are intertwined. Geographer Marco Antonsich describes belonging as a feeling of being "at home" in a place—not physically, but psychologically and socially. So when Sue shared her word, I wasn't surprised. I had been noticing this pattern emerge in my research.

Sue's predicament isn't rare. Many people are searching for their career "place," but they look for it inside the language and logic of career fit—a concept that cannot produce the belonging they crave.

That's because career fit is outdated.

Career belonging is what people are actually longing for.

My Story: A Crisis of Identity, Not Credentials

I understand Sue because I was Sue. My professional identity crisis unfolded over four years, a slow unraveling of everything I believed about who I was and what I was supposed to be in the world of work. On paper, nothing was wrong. My skills, reputation, and qualifications were solid. But I felt lost because I didn't know who I was without a job title to validate my self-worth.

I achieved career fit several times. It's not hard to do when you know how to shapeshift to match what employers want. I landed roles I'm still proud of in higher education, innovation ecosystems, and early childhood development. But eventually, each one left me hollow. I kept wondering: Is it me? The job? The boss? The institution?

Looking back, the answer was none of the above.

I kept choosing roles that fit *just enough*—like clothes you can button and zip, yet never quite flatter your figure. They aren't terrible, but they don't compare to the vibrancy of wearing something that is beautifully tailored to you.

Each role fit me at the time I started, and then eventually it didn't. I brushed this off by saying I outgrew the role or the organization was no longer a fit, but I knew something more was at play. I didn't seem to "fit" anywhere, at least not long term. Five careers in twenty years. My career has zigzagged across education, administration, statewide initiatives, and early-stage startups.

Eventually, I was labeled a job hopper, a "risky" hire. On paper, I did not make sense.

The problem wasn't my lack of a defined path. The problem was the paradigm I was using to interpret who I was.

You see, I'm a hybrid professional, a term I coined to explain someone who weaves multiple professional identities together and works at the intersection of those identities. For me, chasing fit was a dead end. Fit required me to shrink, contort, and translate myself so others would "get me." Over time, I grew exhausted from performing narrow versions of myself.

I wish someone had given me this language years ago, language that would have helped me understand why I never fit neatly into a role, and why chasing fit was the wrong pursuit in the first place. So I'm giving it to you now.

If you're someone who doesn't fit neatly into a box either, then what you're really searching for is a career where you can be fully seen, known, and valued as the sum of your parts.

That's *career belonging*, and millions of people are craving it without knowing what to call it.

Why I Wrote This Book

I've worked with hundreds of people like Sue, and I've been studying the feeling of being a "misfit" in the workforce for more than a decade. That research led to my first book,

More Than My Title, which helped multipotentialites and hybrids articulate who they are beyond job titles.

When hybrid professionals come to me, they start by saying, *"I don't know who I am in my work. I don't know how to share what I do or convey what my unique value is. Nobody gets me."* Once we uncover their true professional identity (who they are beyond their job title), and they embrace that revelation, they inevitably ask the same follow-up question:

> **"Now that I know who I am in my career, where do I fit?"**

This question is asked all the time, especially among women, people with nonlinear career paths, and professionals whose identities defy traditional categories. These are also the same groups who face systemic barriers like bias, misrecognition, and the pressure to continually prove themselves.

As a researcher, I started noticing how often people said, "I don't know where I fit." It came up again and again in interviews, workshops, and coaching sessions, and it eventually sparked this book. Through my research and coaching on professional identity development, I've come to see that the struggle isn't about answering two questions, "Who am I?" and "Where do I fit?" It actually boils down to three deeper questions, which I now call the *Three Career Power Questions*.

Whether we realize it or not, we subconsciously ask ourselves these power questions throughout our careers. These questions form the premise of this book, and by the end, you'll be able to answer them for yourself. They are:

1. ***Who am I in my work (besides my job title)?***
2. ***What does that mean?***
3. ***What makes me feel seen, known, and valued in my career?***

For most of us, these are bewildering questions to answer at first, even existential in nature. We tend to focus on *what we do* for work—our talents, competencies, and problems we solve. However, aligning our work with *who we are* is different. When we focus on our professional identity, that's when we're able to communicate our unique value, and as a result, feel more seen, known, and valued overall.

Who This Book is For

This book is for anyone who feels they don't fit in the workforce and is searching for a better career playbook designed for modern professionals. It's for people who are:

- Feeling unseen, unheard, or misunderstood in their careers (no one gets you).
- Struggling to articulate their unique professional identity and value.
- Ready to embrace their career on their terms.

It's especially for professionals who are **multi-talented, interdisciplinary, or hybrid.** As I've said, *hybrid professional* is my term for people who operate at the intersection of multiple identities simultaneously.

This book is also for **employers, managers, HR leaders, and career coaches** who want to help the types of professionals I just described thrive and advance. If you want to create an environment where talent feels valued for who they are, not just what they do, this book will help you foster that. When professionals feel a sense of career belonging, they are more engaged, more innovative, and more likely to persist. Understanding career belonging can help organizations build stronger workplaces that move beyond outdated professional identity narratives, which limit how people are seen and understood.

The Research Behind Career Belonging

The insights in this book are drawn from five years of field notes and observations from private coaching with over 100 individuals navigating professional identity and career clarity concerns. These engagements included multiple in-depth, one-on-one conversations. In addition, focus groups were conducted with more than 50 professionals across eight countries. Participants represented a wide range of industries, career stages, and life experiences, and shared stories of career frustration, reinvention, and ultimately, belonging.

I also draw from my own background as a researcher and professional identity expert. My methods are rooted in phenomenology, the study of shared lived experiences, and autoethnography, which involves reflecting on my own career journey to uncover broader patterns.

From my research, a consistent truth emerged: **Professionals at all career stages are longing to be seen, known, and valued, but they don't know how to achieve this.**

A meaningful contradiction appeared in the data that ultimately led me to my final insights. Participants commonly said some version of, "Nobody gets me. I don't want to be put in a box," followed closely by, "I just want to find where I fit." Wanting agency while also wanting to belong is a deeply human tension, and it helps explain why so many people don't feel seen in their careers. It's because we've been using the wrong terms to name what we're longing for. This book is my attempt to change that.

What You'll Learn in This Book

By the end of this book, you will understand why career fit is no longer a sufficient framework for meaningful work and why modern professionals need better tools to help them make sense of themselves and their careers. You'll learn:

✓ **Why career fit falls short in the modern workforce**
You'll understand why many professionals feel unseen,

undervalued, or out of place even when they "check all the boxes," and why the language and systems we've inherited haven't kept pace with how people actually work and live today.

✓ **What career belonging really is**
You'll learn how being *seen, known, and valued* forms the foundation of career belonging, and why these three tenets matter more than titles, roles, or resumes when it comes to long-term fulfillment and agency in your work.

✓ **How to define your professional identity beyond a job title**
You'll learn how to articulate who you are in your work in a way that captures your essence, contribution, and multidimensionality, especially if you're a hybrid professional, multipotentialite, or someone who wears many hats.

✓ **A clear framework for moving from fit to belonging**
You'll be introduced to the **Five Steps to Career Belonging**, a structured roadmap that brings the concepts in this book into practice. The steps help you understand where you are now, clarify what's missing, and intentionally shape how you want to experience your career.

✓ **Practical tools to apply career belonging in real life**
Whether you work inside an organization, run your own business, or are in transition, you'll gain tools and language to communicate your value, advocate for yourself, and make choices that align with who you are and how you want to be experienced.

✓ **How to support career belonging in others**
If you're a manager, HR leader, educator, or career coach, you'll learn how to create environments and conversations where people can be seen, known, and valued for who they are, not just what they do.

Importantly, this book contains three layers:

- First, understanding why career fit falls short in the modern workforce.
- Second, giving you the tools and roadmap to achieve career belonging for yourself.
- Third, examining how workforce systems shift when career belonging, not fit, is the goal.

This book is not just about changing how you see yourself, it's about changing how we see each other and how work itself is designed. The career problems we're experiencing are not only personal, they're structural. And if we continue building careers around fit, we will continue misinterpreting people and undervaluing them at scale.

The final part of this book moves beyond the individual because career belonging requires shifts in how we evaluate, recognize, and design work itself. The future of work will not be defined by better talent matching systems or career pathways, but by better identity-based interpretation systems.

There's a powerful undercurrent of dissatisfaction moving throughout the workforce, felt by the employed, self-employed, underemployed, and unemployed alike. People want more than a career that simply pays their bills or comes with decent benefits. They want work where they feel seen, known, and valued for who they are, not just what they do.

This quiet longing, paired with the booming industry of career fit assessments and tools, has led many of us to keep chasing the same promise that career success comes from finding where we fit. But that promise keeps falling short.

It's time we talk honestly about why career fit is overrated, and why so many of us feel lost while doing exactly what we were told to do.

PART ONE

LONGING TO BELONG

CHAPTER 1

Career Fit
Is Overrated

"If the path before you is clear, you're probably on someone else's. You are not on your own path. If you follow someone else's way, you are not going to realize your potential."

—Joseph Campbell

The career fit industry—measured through career counseling and coaching services—was valued at $2.12 billion globally in 2020 and is projected to reach $4.65 billion by 2030. The market for career assessment tools, which includes both online and offline tests designed to help individuals find their fit, was valued at $1.5 billion globally as of 2023, and is expected to reach $3.8 billion by 2032. These staggering figures demonstrate the strong demand for career services aimed at matching people with roles aligned to their skills, values and goals. Essentially, there is *a lot* of money in career matchmaking, and it's not slowing down.

The career services industry is incentivized to sell "fit" because, in two words, it sells! Strong demand doesn't mean what is being sold is the right solution, or that it works long term. Yet, we've been conditioned to believe it does.

It took Yael Gavish nearly seven years to make a big career move on her terms because the pressure she felt to find the right *fit* was holding her back. "The biggest reason I couldn't figure out what I wanted to do was that I was trying to fit into a preexisting box, but none of the preexisting boxes fit me," she wrote. Yael explained she is an artist, technologist, and a writer, and doesn't see a box where all of these things fit together.

That's because there isn't one.

So, Yael quit her job, again, and again tried to make other boxes work. Until one day she embarked on a long journey of introspection that helped her discover what she truly wanted, which ultimately led to a career where she finally felt a sense of belonging. Today, Yael happily creates large-scale minimalist art, writes, and shares her playbook for how she transformed her life. Yael has achieved career belonging.

Yael's aha moment was realizing just how strongly we cling to preconceived notions about ourselves and how we rarely question what's truly possible. That's what led her to changing her own perceptions and listening to her intuition. "Trying to fit into socially approved boxes can make our lives feel flat. Small. Meaningless," she said. Yael's story is not singular.

As part of my initial research for this book, I polled people about their careers. I received many thoughtful responses, but one really stayed with me. CJ Juleff, a business consultant, wrote this poetic phrase:

> I'm curious about the missing state of being, a "career where I am meant to be." I tried to come up with something more clever, but I believe there are many of us who have created a career that allows us to be our authentic selves where we feel fulfilled.

This missing state of being is exactly what I'm talking about. Without knowing what to call it, CJ perfectly articulated what many of us are searching for. There is a space that exists—"career where I'm meant to be"—that is attainable and what many of us are looking for. We just don't know how to reference it collectively. We've been hunting in the dark for this "missing" state, defaulting to calling it "career fit," when it was never about fit at all. It's about something bigger and more complex, something that deeply involves our emotional, psychological, and spiritual needs.

The phrase "career where I'm meant to be" is the essence of career belonging.

Before I go into the facets of career belonging, it is important to unpack why we've been conditioned to seek career fit in the first place, the costs of trying to fit in, and the powerful influence the career fit industry holds over workers and their career paths so we can shift our mindset around this term.

The High Cost of Career Fit

In the introduction, Sue's story exemplifies one of the high costs of career fit—conformity. While Sue liked her employer, took pride in her organization, and held a solid job overall, the pressure to conform to an environment that didn't fully recognize or appreciate her eventually left her burned out and questioning her own abilities.

Even in a dream job, fitting into a role often requires minimizing or suppressing parts of your true self. That's a high cost. It requires you to stifle your creativity, hide your passions, and conform to workplace norms that don't resonate with you. Over time, this kind of suppression can lead to dissatisfaction, disengagement, quiet quitting—or outright quitting—burnout, and even a loss of identity.

Career fit is positioned as a goal to attain. It's defined as the alignment between an individual's skills and traits with the requirements of a job or the needs of the market. It relies on the idea that if you perfectly match your abilities with the right position, you will be successful and satisfied. That's why it has been the constant career north star, shaping everything from degree programs and career pathways to promotions and talent management strategies. Yet in practice, career fit often falls short.

Why? Because career fit is inherently limited. It focuses narrowly on external factors—like job descriptions, skill sets, and market demands—while overlooking the internal landscape of emotional, psychological, and spiritual needs that drive long-term satisfaction and engagement.

After all, you can find a job that perfectly matches your abilities and values, and still feel disconnected, uninspired, or unfulfilled. Career fit doesn't address the deeper question of whether your work resonates with *who* you are as a person. Another cost to pay.

Take the case of Bethany Crystal who used to describe her career as a series of jobs that never quite felt right. She had the skills, the drive, and the adaptability to succeed in different roles, but something always felt off.

Bethany put it best in her ebook, *Go Solo*:

> Up until recently, I've largely pursued
> a career of full-time jobs, one at a time,
> often staying for 3-5 years at a time.
> But I've never held a single job that I'd
> describe as a "perfect fit."

I studied journalism, but I didn't want to
be a journalist. I took a job in sales, but
I spent all my time writing marketing
collateral. I worked at a venture capital
firm, but never actually felt like a VC. So
the pattern continued. I'd work one job at
a time, pour everything I had into it, then
overexert myself to the point of exhaustion and wonder why I felt such a disso-
nance between my "work self" and my
"everything else self."

Bethany wasn't struggling because she lacked direction. She was struggling because she was a hybrid profes- sional—someone who integrates multiple work identities rather than fitting neatly into a single box. Yet for years, she tried to force herself to fit, downplaying parts of her professional self to meet the expectations of each role.

In her blog, *Hard Mode First*, Bethany writes prolifi- cally about being a fractional worker—a professional who thrives by working across multiple fields rather than being confined to a single position. At one point, she even created a graphic to express all the professional identities she saw in herself: Startup Guru, Community Strategist, Blogger, Podcaster, Social Impact Specialist, and more. In the graphic, each identity was crossed out except for the words at the bottom, circled in red: "All of the above."

MY WORK IDENTITY

Go-To-Market Generalist
Startup Guru
Community Strategist
Social Impact Specialist
Venture Capitalist

Professional Networker
Blogger & Podcaster
Education Thought Leader
Just a person who gets stuff
done...?

ALL OF THE ABOVE!

Bethany Crystal's Work Identity Graphic.

That phrase captures what so many professionals feel but can't articulate: they aren't one thing. They are all of the above. For years, Bethany believed she had to choose one identity at a time to be successful. But when she finally let go of the need to "fit" into a predefined career, and instead embraced her hybridity, she unlocked her career belonging.

In 2025, Bethany reached another turning point. She was no longer content with juggling multiple roles as separate projects. Instead, she sought to integrate them into one cohesive career container. That looked like possibly launching her own company, or designing a role that allowed her to fully express all her identities at once. This was a major milestone in her career belonging journey.

This pattern is common among hybrid professionals. At first, they struggle with divergence—moving between roles, never feeling fully at home. But then comes the moment of convergence—when they stop choosing between identities and begin synthesizing them into something new. Bethany stood at that threshold.

Bethany's journey proves that career belonging isn't about finding one perfect job, it's about embracing your multidimensional self in your work and building a career that honors it. At the end of the day, Bethany's desire wasn't to fit into a job description. It was to be accepted and valued for who she truly is. And that's what career belonging is all about.

It's clear that the push to find "career fit" caused Sue, Yael, and Bethany to move on and change careers because they craved something more. Not another skill or challenge, but a way of being in the work world that did not make them sacrifice their sense of self. The cost of maintaining and sustaining career fit was toxic and draining for each of them. When they let go of society's mandate to find career fit and reset what they were truly looking for, it opened them up to other possibilities. That's when they stumbled into career belonging.

The Flawed Promises of Career Fit

Career fit can feel like a triumph at first. When you land a job that matches your skills and qualifications, there's often a sense of relief—even excitement. But over time, the novelty wears off, and you may start questioning the deeper purpose of your work. That's because career fit prioritizes meeting external expectations over nurturing growth and alignment with your evolving identity. A company wants you to be what they need, rather than supporting who you are becoming.

Another cost is that career fit can and does lead to stagnation. When you focus solely on finding a role that matches your current abilities, you miss opportunities for exploration and self-discovery. You become confined by the limits of your job description, unable to expand or innovate beyond the boundaries set by others.

Nicholas Whitaker knows this firsthand. Early in his career at Google, he thrived. He brought news and media products to global outlets. The role made him an international representative of the company, and his expertise was valued. But constant travel and high-pressure demands led to a major panic attack that forced him to reevaluate his work.

A new opportunity for him in Learning & Development seemed like a better fit, on paper. But once in the role, the mismatch became clear. The team dynamics, leadership style, and narrow scope of work left him feeling constrained. Stress took a toll on his mental health, and he eventually took a three-and-a-half-month leave of absence to recover.

When he returned, it was near the start of the COVID-19 pandemic and two things happened. First, he received a low performance review and could see he was being pushed out. Second, he continued putting energy into hosting mental health and mindfulness programs at Google. Something he started before taking leave and even had a budget to host wellbeing events. As the lead volunteer for the G-Pause community, he grew the initiative to support 5,000 employees worldwide during the pandemic.

This work, though not part of his job description, gave him a sense of purpose and belonging—something aligned with who he actually was. Employees started reaching out to him, thanking him for his efforts and appreciating his gifts.

Then came the layoff.

Nicholas's story illustrates the temporary nature of career fit and how flawed it can be. While it can provide benefits, they're often short term, and it rarely meets our deeper needs that lead to long-term fulfillment.

Another flawed promise is that hard work will eventually lead to the right role, promotion, or career. But in reality, many people never get there because the system doesn't always reward the most qualified. Maybe you've watched a less experienced colleague get promoted or been told you're "not quite ready" despite years of results. When this happens, it's easy to think you're missing something, but the real problem may be that you're forcing a fit where there is none. Instead of trying harder to reach a fit, it might be time to question the fit itself. It may never be the right fit for you. Instead, it may be time to start pursuing career belonging.

Remember, the stakes are high when we choose career fit over career belonging.

So, What is a Career Anyway?

Before we move on, let's clear something up. When we use the word "career," not everyone has the same reference point. In fact, the term "career" has become quite messy. My husband has both a JD and an MBA, which means he has a law and business degree, and you'd think this would make his career crystal clear. Yet when I asked him to define his career one day, he looked me in the eye and said, "I don't even know what a career is." Point taken.

Today, the modern "career" is a fluid, hard-to-pin-down idea. It means something different depending on who you talk to. There is no longer a one-size-fits-all definition. The formal definition of a career from the Oxford dictionary is, "an occupation undertaken for a significant period of a person's life and with opportunities for progress." It comes from the Latin word *carrus*, which means "chariot or wheeled vehicle." The etymology shows that the word *career* was originally associated with a racecourse. Obviously, most of us are not following a "course" or finding clear opportunities for progress or upward mobility. This definition is out of sync with contemporary beliefs and standards.

Historian Steven Mintz notes that the traditional concept of a career—linear, predictable, and tied to a single employer—has given way to more varied and dynamic career paths. The modern career is no longer about loyalty to one company or climbing a corporate ladder. It's about crafting a journey that aligns with your personal growth, interests, and values.

As Mintz observes, "We live in an era in which careers have become fragmented, episodic, and deeply personalized." This explanation highlights why the old model no longer resonates with modern workers and why we need a new way of understanding careers.

My assessment is that the only person who can make meaning of and give purpose to your career is you! Full stop. And if you believe this too, then you're probably someone who balks at the false promises the career fit industry sells: that you must shape who you are for the system to accept you.

Of the people I interviewed for this book, most of them don't even believe in the term *career* anymore. Harris Rollinger, a thirty-year-old who transitioned from working in small nonprofits to a large corporation, put it this way:

> I find the definition of a career no longer
> really exists for me. I don't even know
> what it is, which causes anxiety. And I
> feel like I'm trying to push away from the
> definitions that my family and my culture
> and my friends have in order to advocate
> for what I believe. So, I don't have a

definition of a career, and my parents have no idea what I do.

Stephanie Schmitz echoed a similar struggle:

> In my family, a career was a job. Career was the thing that took my family away from me in my childhood. . . .A career was whatever quelled my anxiety and uncertainty. A career was whatever provided security and something that was easy to see and build, something without having to feel lost or have the challenge of creating a brand new path.

It's clear that the term *career* has become a confusing tangle of opinions and projections. When I facilitate discussions about the term *career*, eventually someone says, "We need a new word." Immediately, heads nod in furious agreement. Then, we try to brainstorm what it could be. As hard as we've tried, we haven't found something better yet. One of my interviewees said, "the best way to change it is to stop using it. That's how language evolves." And, that's a radical idea I pose to you. What if we stopped using the term *career* altogether?

The Essence of A Modern "Career"

There are shared beliefs around what people want a modern career to be. Tracy Borreson, a former marketing executive turned authentic marketing advisor, has begun seeing her career in a more personal way:

> My definition of career has become more related to me as an individual. What do I consider meaningful? What do I consider *my* contribution, not just a contribution? I'm getting closer to what that is. I'm definitely still building towards the final answer, but my definition right now is more centered on me than centered on what a "good career" is supposed to look like.

I like to use this definition to describe a modern career:

> ***A modern career is the constellation of meaningful events and experiences over your lifetime that you consider to be part of your work (like an oeuvre, opus, or body of work). It often only makes sense in retrospect.***

I consider my career to be the curated set of my past work experiences that are meaningful to me. My definition was inspired by the late Donald Super, a leading career development theorist and pioneer. Super was the person who described careers as constellations of experiences—a concept that moves away from rigid, linear models and acknowledges the importance of self-concept. His Life-Career Rainbow Theory suggests that both our sense of self and our careers evolve over time, shaped by our lived experiences. He was the first person to overlay a developmental theory within his career theory to show that as we change, so too do our careers. They have a mutualistic relationship, not a parasitic one. His theory was radical in the 1970s when it was first published, but it feels more timely than ever before.

I've included an image of Super's Life-Career Rainbow Theory. He illustrated eight dimensions of our lives that most people experience: child, student, leisurite, citizen, worker, parent, spouse, and homemaker. He put these dimensions in a rainbow-shape with a timeline arc over them from birth to death to represent lifespan. This shows how each of the key roles we play in life come in and out at different times, yet they overlap each other. It's the big reason our self-concept, our worldviews, and our careers evolve. Everything is interrelated and plays off each other. We can be in multiple dimensions simultaneously.

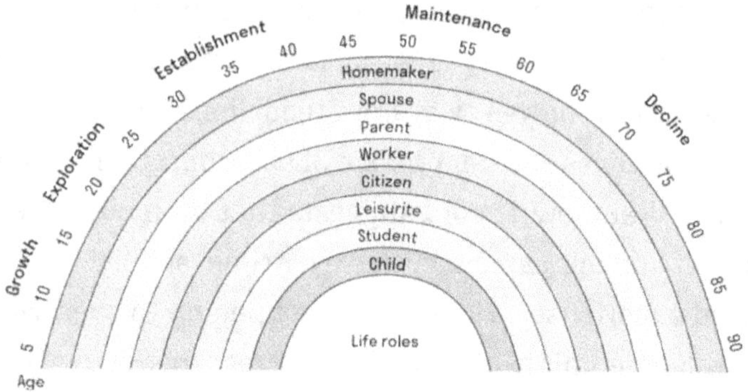

Image Credit: Toolshero.com
Donald Super's Life Career Rainbow.

If I were to condense Super's theory into three questions
to help you reflect on your career today, they would be:

1. What life role(s) are you currently in?
2. What life stage and life cycle are you currently in?
3. What career pattern does this create for you?

Your answers to these questions show how multifaceted a career is. This is the tip of the iceberg in terms of
revealing the overarching narrative you create about your
life's work and who you are in it. When you figure that
out, it becomes the story you tell yourself—and tell to
others—about who you are, what you've navigated, what
you've accomplished, and what you're working toward.
It's hard to fit into a box when you approach your career
with this lens.

The Itch We Really Want to Scratch

Clearly, we've been aiming at the wrong target. Career belonging is the itch we really want to scratch. But, in order to do so, my research shows we don't understand the difference between fit and belonging. When I asked people to define what career fit meant to them, here's a sample of what they said:

- *"A career that's aligned with my skills, values, and lifestyle considerations."*

- *"A feeling of freedom; something that can flow along with my interests and gives me autonomy. It's definitely not a static concept."*

- *"My qualifications match the work requirement."*

- *"I get to bring my zone of genius, array of talents, and authentic self to my role, team, and greater organization. It means I'm progressing on a path of economic mobility that can sustain a family while being valued for who I am at work."*

- *"Feeling at home when at work."*

Only one of these responses—"My qualifications match the requirements"—reflects the true definition of career fit. The rest imply that gnarly itch we've been trying to scratch—career belonging.

We carelessly use the words "fit" and "belong" interchangeably. I'm sure you've swapped them in conversation without giving it a second thought as well. *I don't really fit in. I'm wearing the wrong clothes. People are looking at me funny. I know I don't belong here."* In that context, it's not a big deal to interchange the words "fit" and "belong." But they represent two very different ideas.

Brené Brown explains this perfectly:

> *Fitting in* is about assessing a situation and becoming who you need to be to be accepted. *Belonging,* on the other hand, doesn't require us to change who we are.

If you fit in, you're wearing the clothes others are wearing, you're doing the things others are doing because you want to be accepted. But if you belong, you don't have to wear special clothes or be anything different from who you already are.

That's why career *fit* and career *belonging* require separate career strategies. When my clients say they want to find where they fit and belong in the same sentence, I can tell they don't know they're confused. It's okay because nobody taught them, until now.

An example of career fit looks like this:

> Morgan is a data analyst who has always been good with numbers. She finds a

role in a tech company where her skills in data interpretation and software are highly valued. Her job is stable, and she receives regular promotions. Yet, Morgan feels a lingering dissatisfaction. While her job aligns with her skills, she feels disconnected from her work and yearns for a deeper sense of purpose.

Career fit requires repressing parts of yourself, letting go of traits you love to become a square peg in a square hole. You can do it—we're all capable of fitting in when we choose to—but it doesn't feel good long term. After a while, it weighs on you in unhealthy ways.

An example of career belonging looks like this:

Gerald is a marketing professional with a passion for social justice. He finds a role at a nonprofit organization where he not only uses his marketing skills but also contributes to campaigns that reflect his values. Gerald feels deeply connected to the mission of the organization, and his work brings him a sense of fulfillment and purpose. He feels seen and appreciated not just for his technical skills, but for the passion and creativity he brings to his role.

If we want to transform the broken promises of career fit in today's world, we must first name its limitations and clarify the deeper goal people carry in their hearts and minds: which is to be seen, known, and valued. Those are the core tenets of career belonging as well as the innate qualities we're longing for in a modern career. I will keep reminding you of them.

As you'll see in the chapters ahead, career belonging embodies an enduring sense of agency, autonomy, and connection, and, above all, a strong sense of *self* within your career. By spreading this concept more widely, people will achieve these qualities more readily.

Whether you are like Nicholas, Bethany, or Yael—young or old, just starting your career or evolving it for the fourth, fifth, or sixth time—whether you wear many hats or specialize deeply in one domain, career belonging is possible for everyone.

If you only remember one thing, remember this key point, your career is a constellation that reflects who you are—your identity, your growth, your choices, your journey, your sense of purpose.

Next Steps

- **Reflect**: Where in your career have you tried to "fit" but still felt unfulfilled? What signs have you ignored that pointed toward a deeper need for belonging?

- **Define**: Identify moments where you've paid a high cost for career fit.

- **Do**: Write down two or three career experiences where you felt seen, known, and valued. What made those experiences different?

CHAPTER 2

The New Paradigm of Career Belonging

"Rather than working in a single genre, consider not having a genre. Or combining genres in a way that hasn't been done before."

—Rick Rubin

Are you carving stones or building a cathedral? Think about that for a moment. I want to start with a story you might recognize because it's a famous parable, and it's a perfect way to make my point in this chapter. Leaders often use this parable to inspire teams around building vision, and coaches use it to illustrate the difference between a job, a career, and a calling. I'm using it for a different purpose—to show the distinction between career fit and career belonging, and between professional identity and job titles.

The story goes like this:

> Imagine walking down a beautiful road on a sunny day. As you stroll along, you encounter three people, and each is bent over a gigantic block of stone, hammering away at it.
>
> Curious, you walk over to each person and, one at a time, ask them, "Excuse me, what are you doing?"
>
> The first person replies, "I'm cutting stone. That's my job. I'm a stonecutter."
>
> The second says, "I want to be a master stonecutter. I'm perfecting my craft to become the best in the land."
>
> And the third person answers, "I'm building a cathedral. I'm creating something for the future that will last beyond my time. I'm leaving a legacy for my children and grandchildren."

From the outside, we clearly see three people doing the same work. And, all three have the same job title, that of stonecutter. Yet, all three have different answers to the "what are you doing" question and have a distinct sense of who they are in their work. The first stonecutter is focused solely on the task at hand as a stonecutter. The second has a broader sense of purpose and aims to master their craft. But the third connects the act of cutting stone to something greater: a legacy, a contribution to their community, a lasting endeavor beyond their lifetime.

The only way we learn about each person is by asking them, "What are you doing?" which allows them to share their authentic truth. This causes us to drop our biases, eliminate our assumptions, and perceive more than our observations alone. Through their answers, we change the way we see. We start to see the stonecutters the way they want to be seen, and it transforms our sense of who they are in their work.

The first lesson in this parable is about professional identity—how you see yourself in your work. This lesson asks: *Who are you, really, beyond your job title when you describe what you do?* Just because we see people doing the same task or using the same skills doesn't mean they are the same. And just because we give people the same job title doesn't mean that's what they would call themselves.

I invite you to ponder these questions further:

- How would each stonecutter define who they are in their work besides their job title?

- For what does each stonecutter want to be seen, known, and valued?

- And, how would you find the answers to these questions?

The second lesson is about achieving career belonging over fit. This lesson asks: *Does this work feel like something you merely do, or is it something that is an expression of your true self, others understand that about you, and it's part of something greater?*

When you're merely cutting stones, you're fitting into a role, doing what's required, but not necessarily feeling connected to it or having any agency. When you're mastering your craft, you have a sense that your work serves a purpose and feels fulfilling to practice on a daily basis. Depending on the context, this could be career fit or career belonging. But when you're building a cathedral, your daily work is integral to your life's work, others notice that, and you feel part of something greater than yourself. Building a cathedral isn't just about working on a lifelong endeavor, it's a testament to contributing to something larger and a reflection of who you are in the world.

So, are you trying to carve stones or build a cathedral in your career? Think about it. This is what it means to seek career fit versus career belonging.

Shifting your focus from carving stones to building a cathedral is a new career paradigm. And it requires a new set of career tools to make it possible.

The Essence of Career Belonging

Imagine a career where:

- You are valued not just for your job title or skills, but for **who you are**.

- You can bring your multiple professional identities to work and feel accepted and respected.

- You no longer mold yourself into predefined roles or boxes.

- You have a strong sense of **belonging** by understanding that your career belongs to you, your career is reflected by your colleagues and coworkers, and your career is part of something bigger than you (that could be your community, a movement, an organization, a global issue, or a spiritual or religious force).

Career belonging imbues a feeling of internal and external alignment. Your sense of self in your work is strong and clear and visible to others. It's a space that millions can attain more easily than finding their calling, destiny, or ikigai—those are ultimate labels, a kind of career nirvana, if you will—in their everyday work lives. The same way you can be on a career path or in a career transition, I think of career belonging as a state of being you can inhabit.

I define career belonging this way:

Career belonging is being seen, known, and valued by yourself, others, and something greater than yourself.

This definition intentionally incorporates the three tenets of belonging—feeling seen, known, and valued—and the three levels of belonging—self, others, and something greater than oneself. Together, they form a powerful framework to help us reflect, analyze, and achieve our career desires in a more meaningful and personalized way.

The key differences between career fit and career belonging can be illustrated across five critical aspects of a career: focus, satisfaction, recognition, longevity, and outcomes.

	Career Fit	Career Belonging
Focus	Matching skills and job requirements	Aligning work with values, identity and intuition
Satisfaction	Competence in role	Fulfillment in work and personal growth
Recognition	Valued in job performance	Valued for authentic work self and unique contributions
Longevity	Stable but potentially stagnant	Dynamic and evolving with personal growth
Example Outcome	Regular promotions, but low fulfillment	Deep engagement, purpose, and satisfaction

Notice that career fit is largely driven by external factors, objective attributes, and the fulfillment of basic needs, while career belonging is more self-defined, rooted in connecting your work to your authenticity, values and potential.

Career belonging is the realization that you have more agency over your career than you think, more options than what's immediately visible, and more dimensions of success than you previously imagined. There will always be barriers and external factors that delay or disrupt your path, but if you're striving for career belonging, you must learn to recognize your limiting beliefs and see or even create possibilities you haven't yet perceived.

Two Kinds of Career Belonging

Career belonging is universal, but it isn't experienced the same way by everyone. In fact, there are two primary kinds of career belonging you may recognize yourself in.

The first kind is when your career belongs to an established profession—medicine, law, real estate, design, software engineering, the arts, education, and so on. Your field has a name, a community, and a recognizable identity, and your sense of belonging is tied, at least in part, to the values and definitions designated by that professional body.

The second kind is when your career is *self-defined*—untethered from the norms and conventions of any single field—because you are an N of one. Your identity, contributions, and career path don't fit neatly into established categories, which means the only place your career can truly belong is with you. Despite this difference, the frameworks in this book apply equally well to both paths.

Self-defined career belonging is more complex. It raises more questions, has fewer role models, and doesn't offer a predetermined map to follow. People who experience this kind of belonging are frequently entrepreneurs, creators, independent professionals, or multi-hyphenates, but not always. Some are intrapreneurs or jacks-of-all-trades inside organizations who simply refuse to limit themselves to one lane. Because they don't identify with a single professional group, they often circulate among many communities to stay connected to their full range of interests and identities.

My own career belonging is self-defined. I've never been able to choose a single track because none of them could hold all of me. One of my greatest revelations was recognizing that I have a hybrid professional identity: I work at the intersection of art, education, design, and research. I flourish when I'm able to integrate and move among these circles of thought rather than stay confined to one. In fact, my life force energy depends on my ability to borrow and combine inspiration from multiple domains.

Today, I have a deep sense of who I am and what I bring to the table professionally. I call myself a Creative Disruptor because no matter where I go or what I do, I challenge the status quo and use creativity as a tool for good. As a thought leader, I've begun calling myself a professional identity expert because that is the work I am devoted to.

My career belonging means seeing, knowing, and valuing myself as a Creative Disruptor and professional identity expert, having that reflected by others, and observing that the work I do contributes to something greater than myself. Your version of career belonging may look entirely different, but the feeling—the alignment, the reflection, the sense of self—will be the same.

Workplace Belonging Versus Career Belonging

In Chapter 1, I explained how fluid and expansive the concept of "career" has become, and why it deserves a more modern definition. Since this book centers on *career belonging*, it's important to acknowledge that *belonging* itself is also a broad and multifaceted idea.

We belong to many things across our lives—communities, institutions, identities—and each holds a different weight depending on what we value. For example, belonging to a gym or a church feels different from belonging to your family, and belonging to a workplace is fundamentally different from belonging to your *career*. I want to pause on workplace belonging because my research shows that people often confuse it with career belonging—yet the two are not the same. This confusion is another example of the deep conditioning that leads us to conflate our jobs with our identities.

Workplace belonging is about feeling connected and valued within a specific organization or team. It reflects your relationships with colleagues, the culture you're navigating, and whether you feel included and supported in that particular environment.

Career belonging transcends any single job, workplace, or employer. It is your enduring sense of being seen, known, and valued across the whole arc of your professional life. You can experience career belonging even as you move between roles, companies, industries, or self-employment—what matters is that the work aligns with who you are and what you care about.

In an ideal world, workplace belonging and career belonging would reinforce one another. But they often don't. You might feel deeply connected to a workplace because you enjoy the people and culture, yet the work itself doesn't fulfill you—leaving career belonging out of reach. Conversely, you might find a career path that aligns beautifully with your identity and values, yet struggle to find a workplace that truly recognizes your worth.

Take Laetitia de Haas, for example. She is deeply engaged in her work and feels strong alignment. In fact, she believes she's found her calling as a pioneer of novel approaches in leadership and technology. Her focus on AI and consciousness blends her diverse skills and insights into a purposeful whole, giving her a profound sense of fulfillment. She describes her work as an integral part of her being—no longer divided by traditional boundaries between life and career.

Yet even with this strong sense of career belonging, finding a workplace that embraces and values her cross-disciplinary approach has been difficult. Many organizations struggle to understand or support the depth of her work, leaving her searching for a community or company that truly resonates with her purpose and perspective. This disconnect highlights a reality many people face: you may achieve career belonging, but finding a workplace that matches it can still be elusive.

Understanding the distinction between workplace belonging and career belonging helps you make more informed choices about both your career path and your work environment. It also empowers you to seek out—or even create—spaces where both types of belonging can coexist.

Why Career Belonging Isn't on Employers' Radar

Companies must balance mission, business goals, and financial performance while also managing employee retention, engagement, and satisfaction. Adding "career belonging" to that list isn't even on most employers' radar. To them, it feels like just one more priority competing for attention.

This isn't surprising. Workplace belonging dominates current conversations, especially within Diversity, Equity, Inclusion, and Belonging (DEIB) strategies. These efforts focus on fostering inclusivity *within* an organization's staff. But as I've said, workplace belonging does not automatically create career belonging. These are different types of belonging with different outcomes.

For most of us, advocating for your career needs is your responsibility. If you're craving greater career belonging, you will need to educate your manager, team, or employer about what it is, why it matters to you, and how it ultimately benefits the organization.

Career belonging can be woven into your performance or professional development plan, discussed as a topic within employee resource groups, or introduced during a lunch-and-learn. Find ways to start the conversation and see how it unfolds. My hope is that this book gives you the language and confidence to do exactly that. Chapter 11 provides a detailed list of strategies to try.

More people want careers that bring them a sense of belonging in the work world, yet we also have to play an active role in creating that belonging for ourselves. Everyone faces career changes and setbacks, but without career belonging, the impact on your self-esteem, self-concept, and self-efficacy can cut deeper and take longer to heal—making career transitions or reinventions more challenging.

We seek belonging across every facet of our lives, and we feel the consequences when we don't have it. That's why finding, or reclaiming, career belonging matters so much. It has a measurable and long-lasting impact on our professional success.

Achieving Career Belonging

Achieving career belonging is not a matter of privilege or opportunity, although it can certainly feel that way. I'm not denying that systems of privilege and oppression continue to shape the workforce or that some groups face greater barriers than others. What I *am* saying is that career belonging is not earned through being good enough, prepared enough, or resourced enough. It does not require more time, money, influence, or power.

You already have everything you need to reach career belonging if you choose.

Career belonging requires two things:

1. **Examining, healing, and redefining your beliefs about what a career is**, and
2. **Clarifying and expressing what you need to feel seen, known, and valued**—by yourself, by others, and by something greater than you.

Most of us take these for granted or have never done this inner work before. And even when we think we've defined our beliefs about careers, those beliefs are usually shaped more by cultural conditioning—parents, workplaces, institutions—than by our own truth. Part 3 of this book guides you through a series of steps that will take you deeper into self-examination than you've likely gone before, giving you the tools to reach career belonging on your own terms, if that is your goal.

The benefits of career belonging clearly outweigh the promises of career fit. Career belonging has been the hidden undercurrent millions of people have been longing for without having the language to describe it. Now that we know what to call it—and why it matters—it's time to embrace career belonging, cultivate it, honor it, and make it part of our lives.

But to reach career belonging, you need to know *what* belonging is made of. Belonging isn't a single feeling, it lives at the intersection of feeling seen, known, and valued. It happens when you're observed in practice, interpreted accurately by others, and recognized for your contributions. When all three are present, the experience of career belonging becomes unmistakable.

That's where we're headed next. In the following chapter, we'll explore the Three Tenets of Belonging. Once you understand these, you'll begin to see your career with new clarity and sense what needs to shift.

Next Steps

- **Reflect**: How do the differences between career fit and career belonging resonate with you? Have you ever felt these differences in your own career?

- **Define**: How does workplace belonging differ from career belonging in your experience? Or, identify one area in your career where a lack of career belonging has held you back.

- **Do**: Identify one area in your career where you are currently conforming rather than aligning with your true professional self.

CHAPTER 3

The Three Tenets: Seen, Known, Valued

"Grieve all the versions of you
That tried to shrink
Into spaces that did not belong to you
And then promise
To never do it again."

—Maia

Seen, known, and valued are not just feelings. They are the conditions that make belonging possible. In the last chapter, we named a new paradigm: career belonging. But naming something isn't the same as understanding what it actually requires. At this point, career belonging may still sound abstract or aspirational, so let's better understand what it's actually made of.

When I began researching the topic of belonging, I looked at how it was discussed across psychology, sociology, geography, and organizational studies. While definitions vary by field, the themes remain remarkably consistent. Researchers argue that people experience belonging when they feel accepted, respected, connected, recognized and understood by others, and when they believe they are part of something where they matter, whether that's a group, a profession, a religion, or a movement.

Beneath the surface, these expressions point to the same human needs. People experience belonging when they feel **seen, known, and valued**. This is why I chose this language. These terms capture the core tenets of belonging in a way that is both precise and human. They reflect the observable dimensions of belonging as well as the felt ones, and they show up consistently in the research and in the real language people use.

In my work, I've come to realize that belonging is built from being:

- Seen → **observation**
- Known → **interpretation**
- Valued → **recognition**

Let's look at them one by one to understand how each tenet answers a specific question in regards to belonging as well as how each solves a specific human need.

Being Seen

Asks the question: *Am I visible?*

Being seen refers to what is visible, audible and directly observable. It includes whether you are acknowledged or your voice is heard. You can be in the room and still not be seen. When people say they don't feel seen in their work, they're often describing one or more of the following:

- Being noticed, acknowledged, listened to, heard, visible, understood, and included

Being Known

Asks the question: *Do people actually get me?*

Being known is not how you show up in a moment but about inferences over time. It's shaped by your habits, actions and behaviors. This is where reputation, perception, and relational understanding live. It's about whether others grasp who you are in your work, and whether the way you're understood matches who you believe yourself to be. People describe it this way:

- Being regarded, taken seriously, accurately interpreted, trusted, noted for something, and remembered by reputation

Being Valued

Asks the question: *How am I recognized?*

Being valued is expressed through appreciation, trust, opportunity, and compensation. This tenet reveals whether your presence actually matters in material and relational ways. Valuing becomes unmistakable when it's demonstrated through:

- Being recognized in tangible ways, accepted, respected, sought after, rewarded (financially and non-financially), invested in, cared for, accepted, and proud of one's contribution

Together, these three tenets form the basis of career belonging. When all three are present and aligned, career belonging becomes inevitable and sustainable.

To understand how powerful these tenets really are, it helps to see them in action. Few things illustrate the experience of being seen more clearly than an unexpected moment of recognition. That's what happened in an actual off-Broadway performance that promised it would help the audience "Discover who you really are."

Try this out. Close your eyes, and imagine you're at a theater where, upon entering, you're prompted to select a card that completes the statement, "I am..." The options hanging on the wall in front of you are endless: "I am an activist," "I am a dreamer," "I am a misfit," "I am a healer," "I am a creator," and so forth. Some selections feel safe, while others might hold a secret truth for you. Without realizing it, by choosing an identity word, you've begun your journey into the performance.

This activity is how Derek DelGaudio begins his off-Broadway show *In & Of Itself*. It's a performance that is as much about magic as it is about the human experience. The entire show is a question about the things we see and if they are a distortion of reality or the truth. On stage, Derek shares his own struggles with identity, blending stories, illusions, and deeply personal moments into a captivating performance. His voice is calm but commands attention, drawing you in as he breaks apart labels we carry.

The show isn't about magic tricks or spectacles. It's about how we see ourselves and how the world sees us in return. Derek uses the metaphor of a dog transforming into a wolf to reflect on his own journey. He notes there's a moment each day when the angle of the sun makes it impossible to know if you're seeing a dog or a wolf, a friend or a foe. Derek reminds us we can't always trust our eyes to see things by the right name, a lesson about the nature of seeing. Each act of the performance feels like a mirror, reflecting another layer about our own lives and identities.

Finally, the show reaches its emotional crescendo. Derek begins to call on audience members seated in their rows, and asks them to stand one at a time. To each person, he reveals the identity they chose at the start of the evening. "You are a believer," he says to one. "You are a healer," he says to another. Each time, he gets their word perfectly correct, which is the magic trick.

Even more impressive, as he says these names out loud, something remarkable happens. People begin to tear up and cry, not out of sadness, but because of the power of being seen so clearly. For many, it is the first time they feel genuinely acknowledged, as if a stranger has glimpsed their soul. This is what being seen does. It transforms your very existence. This moment captures the essence of being seen: accurate recognition, offered aloud, without explanation or justification.

In & Of Itself is inspiring because it vividly demonstrates the profound importance of feeling seen, known, and valued right before our very eyes. The impact is undeniable. Recognizing others and recognizing yourself is a gift and a skill to develop. Without it, you can't achieve career belonging. By the way, if you're curious to watch Derek's entire performance, it's available online, and I recommend seeing it for yourself. My husband and I have watched it countless times.

(Scan to watch Derek Delgaudio's *In & Of Itself*)

Skills Not Traits

What happens on that stage looks like magic. But it isn't. It's the result of precise seeing, deep knowing, and intentional valuing, and those are skills. What most of us miss is that seeing, knowing, and valuing are **skills**, not personality traits.

We tend to assume they're innate, that people either do them well or they don't. But what I've learned from my coaching is like any meaningful skill, they can be practiced, strengthened, and refined.

Before you can be seen, known, and valued in your career, you have to learn how to see, know, and value yourself and others. The better you get at that, the more fluently you'll be able to articulate and activate career belonging. I'll go through them one at a time to provide practical tools and tips on how to see, know, and value. These will be useful later on when you're ready to become seen, known, and valued in Chapter 11.

Learning to See

I have two degrees from art schools, and my undergraduate degree is in Visual and Critical Studies. As an artist, I've been learning ways of seeing for years. I didn't realize how unique this skill was until I started working in business environments that prioritize communication, problem-solving, and organizational efficiency. I saw firsthand how the skill of "seeing" wasn't something we discussed. In fact, it was neglected entirely.

When I was an art student, I had the privilege of studying with Professor James Elkins who challenged us not to trust our eyes but to question our vision. He wrote the book, *The Object Stares Back: On the Nature of Seeing.* We analyzed every inch of a photograph, painting, or sculpture to look beyond its surface and see what it really represented.

In his book, Elkins defines seeing as an active, complex, and reciprocal process. When we look at an object, the object "looks back" at us, meaning that our act of seeing is influenced by what we are observing. He emphasizes that seeing involves a dynamic exchange between the seer and the seen. Seeing is also inherently selective. What we notice is shaped by emotional state, cultural conditioning, and psychological filters.

Likewise, John Berger, another influential art critic, wrote the seminal book *Ways of Seeing.* He argued that looking, or "gazing," is never neutral, and that how we see is shaped by power structures in society, such as class, gender, and ideology. By questioning these forces, we gain a more grounded understanding of ourselves in the world and in our careers.

To learn how to see, here are a few strategies:

- **Question What You're Looking At:** Don't take your self-image—or the person you're looking at—at face value. Analyze the assumptions behind what you're looking at. Just because someone wears certain jewelry, has a particular haircut, or displays specific body language or demeanor, ask yourself: Who benefits in the job market the way you or someone else is presenting themselves? There is more happening under the surface of what you see.

- **Understand Your Context**: What we see gains meaning through context. How you see yourself or someone in a setting or on social media can shift its interpretation. We're all familiar with how filters are used to portray idealized versions of humanity.

- **Recognize Power Structures**: Be aware that what you see is shaped by dominant ideologies. For example, corporate environments often prioritize traits like assertiveness and constant availability as markers of leadership—overlooking quieter forms of influence, such as active listening or thoughtful reflection. Recognizing these biases helps you question whether you're conforming to expectations that don't align with your authentic self.

- **Cultivate Curiosity:** Engage with yourself and others with curiosity rather than judgment. This allows for more than one interpretation and a deeper connection with what you observe. Instead of making assumptions, ask yourself, *"What might* *be influencing my behavior that I don't see?"* This question opens the door to empathy and self-understanding, helping you move beyond the surface.

As you practice seeing, stay mindful of what you see, how you see it, and how you've come to see it over time. Quick thought experiment: Think about a coworker or colleague. How do you see them? How have you come to see them over time? How has context shaped your observations of them? Notice what you're noticing about your own observations of that person (this is the meta-awareness part of seeing).

By recognizing that seeing involves more than just our eyes, and questioning what our vision tells us, we gain deeper insights into ourselves, our subconscious, and our conditioned perceptions. The process of seeing becomes a massive tool for self-exploration and growth, career reflection as well as for empathy building.

Learning to Know

How does someone come to "know" you? What are you known for? We say the words "I've known him since he started here," but what does it mean to "know" someone? How do we do this? It's not just the facts we collect: where they've worked, what they do, how they spend their time, what their skills are, or what their career history is. It's about something deeper, understanding what drives them, what matters to them, and how they see themselves and their career.

Learning to "know" requires making educated inferences over time. To truly know yourself and others, you must listen beyond words, observe patterns in behaviors, and understand what genuinely matters to both of you. The same applies to becoming known. Notice what your daily actions communicate about you. Are you intentional and consistent about the way you engage, collaborate, and contribute?

Brené Brown, in *Daring Greatly*, teaches that being "known" is rooted in being authentic. She argues that allowing yourself to be vulnerable—revealing your true self to others—fosters trust and deep connections. Knowing is understanding the impression you make and how others experience you besides your job title. It's the way you show up in a room, the energy you bring, and the values you consistently embody.

Others know you not just for what you do, but how you do it. The way you handle challenges, how you treat people when no one is watching, and the unique presence you bring to every interaction are how you're known. As Maya Angelou famously said, "I've learned that people will forget what you said, people will forget what you did, but people will never forget how you made them feel." They will talk about your integrity, your generosity, and your ability to listen long after you leave. Your reputation, the way others describe you when you're not in the room, is shaped by these intangible qualities.

To learn how to know, here are a few strategies:

- **Notice the Energy You Bring:** Pay attention to how others respond to your presence. Do people seek you out for support, new ideas, or perspective? Do they hesitate to approach you? The way you engage in conversations, navigate challenges, and contribute to group dynamics shapes how others perceive and experience you.

- **Observe How Others Describe You:** Your reputation is more than your job title, it's built on the qualities people associate with you. Listen to how colleagues introduce you or refer to your contributions. Are you known for your reliability, creativity, or ability to bring people together? If what you hear doesn't match how you want to be known, consider how your actions and words can shift that perception.

- **Be Intentional About What You Reinforce:** People remember consistent patterns, not isolated moments. If you want to be known as someone who fosters collaboration, make a habit of acknowledging and amplifying others' ideas. If you want to be seen as a strategic thinker, regularly share insights that connect the dots. What you repeatedly do shapes how people know and remember you. Author James Clear writes all about this in his book *Atomic Habits*.

- **Focus on the Moments That Matter:** The smallest gestures—like offering help without being asked, remembering personal details, or expressing genuine appreciation—often make the greatest impact. These simple acts create a sense of being known and strengthen the connections that shape your professional presence.

Knowing is about understanding the impact you have on others through your daily actions and intentionally shaping that impression with clarity and consistency. When you develop this skill, you don't just wait for people to figure out who you are, you guide the narrative through your actions, your presence, and the way you show up in the world.

Learning to Value

While seeing and knowing focus on observations and interpretations, valuing is about honoring worth, both in yourself and others. In a career context, valuing means recognizing the intrinsic importance of contributions, skills, ideas, and experiences, while also appreciating diverse professional identities. In practice, valuing often shows up in who gets stretch opportunities, who is trusted with ambiguity, and whose work is resourced rather than merely praised.

Psychologist Carl Rogers, a pioneer of humanistic psychology, emphasized the concept of unconditional positive regard. He argued that valuing someone shouldn't depend on their achievements or conformity but rather on seeing them as inherently worthy. Applied to careers, this philosophy encourages us to value ourselves and others not just for what we achieve but for who we fundamentally are.

Similarly, Adam Grant, in *Give and Take*, explores how valuing others fosters collaboration and growth. Grant's research shows that professionals who adopt a "giver" mindset, prioritizing the success and contributions of others, tend to build thriving networks and foster positive workplaces. These perspectives remind us that valuing is an active process requiring intention and thoughtfulness.

To learn how to value, here are a few strategies:

- **Start with Self-Compassion and Affirm Your Worth:** Before you can value others, you must value yourself. Kristin Neff, a leading researcher on self-compassion, emphasizes the importance of treating yourself with kindness, particularly during moments of failure or self-doubt. Practice affirming your worth regularly. Instead of saying, "I'm not good enough for this role," reframe it as, "I bring unique strengths and perspectives to this work."

- **Recognize Contributions Beyond Results:** Valuing isn't only about what's tangible. Take time to appreciate non-quantifiable contributions like emotional intelligence, creativity, and mentorship. When reflecting on your work, ask yourself: "What aspects of my effort made a difference beyond the measurable outcomes?" Similarly, acknowledge these qualities in others to foster a culture of appreciation.

- **Engage in Active Gratitude:** Expressing gratitude is one of the most potent ways to value yourself and others. Create moments to thank yourself and coworkers for their unique contributions. For example: "I appreciate the way you approached that challenge. It added a perspective I wouldn't have considered." Research on gratitude shows that receiving appreciation, especially when it's specific and unexpected, has a powerful emotional impact. People consistently underestimate how meaningful their words of gratitude will be to others. For the person receiving it, being genuinely appreciated often creates a lasting sense of recognition and worth.

- **Challenge Biases and Systemic Inequities:** As mentioned earlier, questioning power dynamics and social norms is key to "seeing" clearly. It also applies to valuing by asking: "Why don't I feel valued in my work, and how can I change that?" "Who else might not feel valued, and how can I help them?" and, "What systems or structures make some contributions more visible than others, and how can I advocate for more equity?"

Learning to value means developing a mindset that acknowledges the worth of every individual, including yourself. Like seeing and knowing, valuing isn't passive, it requires intention, empathy, and consistent action. It's about actively recognizing contributions that might otherwise go unnoticed, whether it's your own quiet strengths or the subtle impact others make in your work and life.

From Learning to Being

Seeing, knowing, and valuing are practices to be learned. Career belonging begins when these three skills move from theory into action, and from action into daily patterns. That's why you'll create a set of personalized Seen Known Valued Statements in Step 5 of this process.

In the next chapter, we'll explore *where* belonging is experienced: within yourself, in relationship with others, and in connection to something greater than yourself. These are the three levels of belonging. Together, the tenets and levels form the full architecture of career belonging.

Next Steps

- **Reflect**: How strong are your skills in seeing, knowing, and valuing? Which comes most naturally to you, and which do you need to develop further?

- **Define**: Notice the way you present yourself in a meeting or interaction to better align with how you want to be known.

- **Do**: Observe how others experience you. What do your actions communicate? How do colleagues describe you? What patterns do you notice in how you show up?

CHAPTER 4

The Three Levels: Self, Others, Something Greater

*"To feel as if you belong
is one of the great triumphs of human existence–
and especially to sustain a life of belonging
and to invite others into that."*

—David Whyte

When I first came across a framework called *The Three Levels of Belonging*, I literally said out loud, "Where has this been? And why don't more people know about it?"

I found it in the *Journal of Spirituality in Mental Health*, authored by Australian researchers Neil and Penny Barringham. They developed it through years of community-based work with people who had been socially isolated, institutionalized, or disconnected from their communities due to mental health challenges. What struck me immediately was how simple yet profound it was.

They proposed that belonging isn't one-dimensional. It operates on **three distinct but interconnected levels**:

- belonging to self
- belonging to others
- belonging to something greater than self

Reading this framework reframed everything I thought I knew about belonging. It created a more expansive view. More importantly, it revealed what's been hidden from how we talk about our careers. So I adapted it.

What emerged is what I now call **The Three Levels of Career Belonging, which include**:

1. Self
2. Others
3. Something greater than yourself

Another way to say this as a statement is:

> Your career belongs to you, is reflected by others, and is part of something greater than yourself.

Most career frameworks only address one of these levels. At best, two. Almost none help you hold all three at once. That's why so many people feel successful *and* dissatisfied at the same time.

First Impressions of the Three Levels

Pause for a moment. What is your first impression of the Three Levels of Career Belonging? What stands out to you?

Before I explain what they mean, I want you to notice what comes up for you instinctively. What do these three levels represent for you? What feels familiar? What feels surprising?

It's unlikely you'll have immediate answers, although you might. These levels tend to get your wheels turning because they invite a kind of reflection you're probably not used to applying to your career. They're novel, and novelty has a way of waking us up.

Consider the following questions:

- Which level of career belonging do you feel most anchored in right now?
- Which level feels least developed or hardest to access?
- Which one surprises you, or isn't something you've consciously thought about before?

When I posed these questions to a diverse focus group, most participants initially believed their sense of career belonging came primarily from within themselves. They saw themselves as being in the driver's seat of their career.

Yet, the level that consistently surprised people, and sparked the most discussion, was the idea that *your career is part of something greater than yourself*. It was the obvious-but-overlooked level. People hadn't realized how little space they'd given it, or how much it might matter.

What surprised them is exactly what surprised me.

For a long time, I believed my career belonging was created by forces outside of me. I assumed it was shaped by pedigree and proximity, by the reputation of the institutions I'd worked for, the titles I held, my family background, and the social capital I had access to, along with external forces beyond my control, like the economy, employer preferences, social trends, and market demands.

What I eventually realized is that I had been outsourcing my sense of career belonging. Before I could be seen, known, or valued by anyone else, I needed to reclaim the relationship I had with myself and my work. This is why the first level of career belonging begins with self.

Let's examine them one at a time. Each level matters on its own, but career belonging emerges from how these levels interact, not from perfecting any single one.

Level One: Career Belonging and Self

How does your career belong to you? This level is about connection to self. It's about understanding what you want, what you need, and how you define your career from your own truth, rather than defaulting to the expectations others placed on you. Essentially, your career belongs to you. While you don't control every circumstance, you do have agency over how you inter-pret your experiences, make meaning of your work, and decide what you're moving toward.

Your connection to self is fueled by your lived experiences but also by intuition, those moments of clarity that emerge when you trust your gut to reveal what aligns with your core values. It requires deep, even radical, self-awareness and self-acceptance to be able to trust your intuition. Before you can feel career belonging in the external world, you must first cultivate it within yourself by understanding who you are, what you stand for, and defining what your career means to you.

I think of this level as the place where you wake yourself back up to yourself. You unearth forgotten desires, listen for the voice that's been buried under expectation, and rebuild trust in your own inner knowing. You remind yourself that you know what you want, you know what you're good at, and you're allowed to define your career on your own terms.

At this level, you must reflect your unique vantage point on the world back to yourself so you can remember what kind of life you want to live and lead. Reminding yourself of this is hard when you're constantly deluged by outside depictions of what you're "supposed to" be. For me, "waking myself back up to myself" in terms of my career has meant reclaiming my professional identity, knowing, deep down, who I am and the value I possess and provide, and turning those into mantras I can repeat and remember. But belonging to self is just one step. Careers don't exist in isolation, and neither do we.

Level Two: Career Belonging and Others

Where and when is your career reflected by others in a way that shows the truth, not a distortion of the world around you? Once your career begins to belong to yourself, something else becomes unavoidable: you start to notice how others respond to you.

Career belonging is reflected back to us through people: through managers, colleagues, clients, industries, and communities, as well as through systems: workforce pathways, applicant tracking systems, performance management tools, hiring processes, resumes and AI filters.

This second level of career belonging asks a different set of questions: *How am I understood? How am I interpreted? And by whom?*

"Others" is a big word. Start by defining what *others* means to you. It can include your current and past employers, coworkers, customers, family members, community, market forces, AI tools or any other influences you choose. It could also mean your career belongs to a traditionally defined field or occupation. There are no fixed rules for what "others" means. It's contextual, relational, and shaped by the career you're building.

For some people, belonging to others shows up as membership in a clearly defined profession. Being a doctor, engineer, or attorney often means belonging to associations, institutions, or communities with shared norms, values, and expectations. These groups signal what is rewarded, what is respected, and what "counts" as success. The question at this level is not whether these norms exist, but how much you actually align with them.

I experienced this tension firsthand when I worked in K–12 education. There were two dominant camps: educators who believed deeply in standardized testing, and those who challenged it. As an art educator, I advocated for portfolios and nontraditional forms of assessment that honored creativity and multiple ways of demonstrating learning. While I shared many values with the education profession, I did not share all of them. As a result, my sense of career belonging was limited. I felt connected to a niche group of educators and alienated from the greater profession.

This is an important distinction. Level two career belonging does not require total alignment. In fact, many people experience belonging through selective resonance—finding pockets of shared values within a larger system that may not fully reflect who they are.

If you don't have a traditionally defined occupation, or if your career spans multiple identities, you are not at a disadvantage here. You simply belong differently. As a jack-of-all-trades or hybrid professional, you may belong to multiple communities at once, or move fluidly between them. You might find belonging in interdisciplinary spaces rather than within a single professional box.

That's why spaces like SXSW and TED events exist. They aren't organized around one profession, but around intersections: technology and culture, science and storytelling, ideas and action. As the workforce becomes less linear and less easily categorized, new forms of professional belonging are emerging to meet people where they actually are.

At this level, career belonging is shaped by relationships. It's influenced by who reflects you accurately, who misunderstands you, and where your contributions are recognized or overlooked. Understanding this level helps you see where belonging is being reinforced, where it's being constrained, and where you may need to choose alignment intentionally rather than by default.

Even when this level is strong, something can still feel unfinished. Your career can belong to yourself, and it can be understood and respected by others, but you can still feel like something is missing. That's because careers don't only live inside us or between us. They also live across time, impact, and meaning. This is where the third level of career belonging comes in.

Level Three: Career Belonging and Something Greater Than Yourself

What am I serving beyond myself or my coworkers in the work I do? What does my work mean beyond me? Level

Three is not about discovering your purpose or finding your calling. It's about understanding the context your career lives inside of. It asks how your work participates in something beyond your individual role or lifespan, whether that's a team, a profession, a community, an era, or a shared human need.

"Something greater" can take many forms. It might be philosophical, social, cultural, generational, spiritual, or civic. Your career might contribute to a movement, a cause, a field of knowledge, or a future you may never fully see. This level is not about ego or ambition. It's about contribution, continuity, and impact.

For some people, this shows up through activism or social change. For others, it's about stewardship, mentorship, or building something that lasts. It can be local or global. Visible or quiet. What matters is not scale, but significance.

This level often goes unnamed in career conversations. We're taught to think about success in terms of individual advancement, growth, or external validation. Rarely are we invited to ask how our work fits into a greater arc, or what it gives back beyond personal gain.

Personally, this level has become increasingly important to me over time. I think a lot about how my work contributes to audiences beyond my own network as well as to future generations. I care deeply about creating things that outlive me in meaningful ways. That's one of the reasons I wrote my first book. I wanted to put something into the world that could travel farther than I could, reach people I would never meet, and offer language where there was once confusion.

When someone reaches out to tell me that my work helped them articulate something they couldn't name before, I feel this level of belonging immediately. In those moments, my career is no longer just a series of outputs or accomplishments. It transcends space and time. That's what this level is about.

This third level also changes how we relate to success. It shifts the focus from accumulation to contribution, from recognition to resonance. It invites us to consider not just what we do, but why it matters, and to whom.

It's important to point out that you do not need a calling, a grand purpose, or a lifelong mission to experience this level of career belonging. You only need to understand how your work fits into a broader context beyond yourself.

Career belonging becomes most real and sustainable when all three levels are present in your life. Without this level, work can feel transactional or self-contained. With it, your career becomes part of a larger story, one that gives your efforts context, weight, purpose and direction.

Conceptualizing the Three Levels

At this point, you might be tempted to assume the three levels of career belonging are linear or sequential. First your career belongs to yourself, then it's reflected by others, and finally it's part of something greater. That interpretation makes sense, especially in a culture that loves stages, ladders, and progressions.

But that's not how this framework actually works.

The three levels are relational. They can exist simultaneously, unevenly, or in different proportions depending on the season of your life and career. How you imagine them matters, because it reveals how you experience career belonging in practice, not just in theory.

Before I show you a few diagrams that represent the three levels, I want you to try something. If you had to draw the three levels of career belonging, what would they look like?

- Would they be balanced?
- Would one dominate the others?
- Would they be nested, overlapping, or distant?
- Would they change depending on the moment you're in?

Go ahead. Draw something. Don't fret about what you draw. The act of drawing forces you to externalize something you've likely never been asked to articulate. It surfaces your unconscious beliefs about the levels: which ones you prioritize, which ones are underdeveloped, and which ones may be shaping your decisions quietly, without your awareness.

When I shared my first diagram of the three levels with a focus group, I expected agreement. Instead, they challenged it immediately. People pushed back on the proportions, the order, and even the shapes. What started as critique turned into insight. Disagreement was the point. Each person was revealing how they experience the levels of belonging in their own life.

That insight led me to treat the levels as a **set of possible configurations**. Below are a few ways people visualize the three levels of career belonging. None of these are better than the others. They're simply different ways of making sense of the core idea.

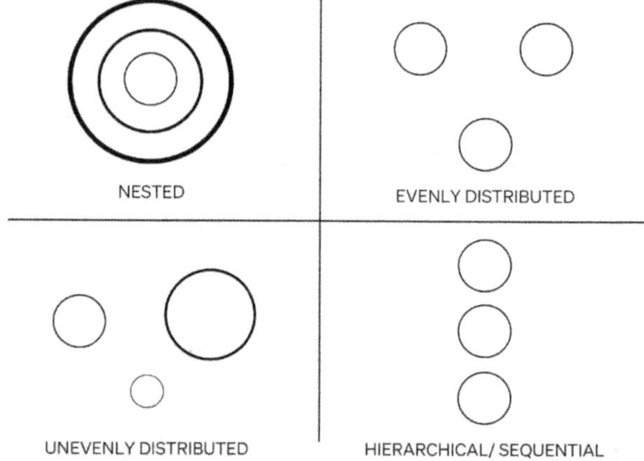

As you can see, some people experience the levels as nested, with self at the center and the other levels radiating outward. Others see them as equally weighted, each holding similar importance. Some experience them unevenly, with one level dominating at a particular stage of life. Others see them as sequential or developmental, shifting emphasis over time.

Only you know which depiction feels accurate for you.

This is one reason conversations about career belonging can feel confusing at first. We don't share a common mental map. You didn't even know these three levels existed until a few pages ago.

By contrast, if I asked you to visualize career fit, you'd likely reach for the same metaphors as millions of others: a square peg in a square hole, a key in a lock, a hand in a glove. Career fit is easy to picture because it's rigid and singular. Career belonging is harder to visualize because it's relational and dynamic.

This is where the three levels of career belonging opens into something deeper. Jungian philosopher James Hollis asks two enduring questions:

- *What is the nature of your relationship with your inner life?*
- *What is the nature of your relationship with the people around you?*

The three levels of career belonging speak directly to these philosophical questions. They invite you into an existential relationship with your career, not just a strategic one. Career fit asks whether you match a role. Career belonging asks whether your work is an expression of you, how well that is reflected by others, and what you are truly part of.

Without this philosophical shift, it's easy to treat careers as a zero-sum game: winning or losing, climbing or falling, achieving or failing. Hollis describes this as the "terrible paradox" of modern life, where people reach the top (of a career ladder) only to discover there's no there there.

Preparing for What's to Come

You now have the full framework for understanding career belonging: the **three tenets** (seen, known, valued) and the **three levels** (self, others, something greater).

You can now see how this book is asking you to think about your career in a way that most never invite. Instead of narrowing you toward a role or title, career belonging opens the aperture. It asks you to consider not just *what you do*, but how your work relates to who you are, how you're reflected by others, and what your career contributes beyond you.

Let these ideas settle. Notice what resonates. Notice what challenges you. The work ahead is about giving you structure, language, and tools to turn all of these ideas into action.

In Part 2, we'll move toward actively building career belonging. You'll work through a five-step process designed to help you clarify your professional identity and articulate how you want to be seen, known, and valued across all three levels. The central tool in the five-step process is the Career Belonging Matrix, which brings the tenets and levels together into a single, practical framework for reflection.

Before you begin building career belonging through the five steps, you need a way to orient yourself. You need to surface how well you already see who you are, what's missing, and what's been difficult to name. The next chapter introduces three career power questions that do exactly that.

Next Steps

- **Reflect**: Which level of career belonging feels most present in your life right now: self, others, or something greater? Which feels least developed?

- **Define**: In your own words, what does career belonging mean to you at each level? Aim for honesty over precision.

- **Do**: Sketch the way you see the three levels of career belonging in your own life. Understanding how you conceptualize them is a practical exercise. The way you imagine them shapes how you make decisions, where you seek validation, and what you prioritize when something feels off in your career.

CHAPTER 5

The Three Career Power Questions

"Our study [on belonging] sought to make people feel less like a ship lost at sea and more like co-travelers taking the first steps on a journey full of possibility."

— Geoffrey Cohen

How many times a week are you asked, "What do you do?" And, how often do you answer with your job title, your organization, or the key problems you sovle—mostly because you don't know what else to say? Maybe you deflect the question entirely because it feels too basic, too obtuse, or too disconnected from who you actually are.

I've come to believe that the *"What do you do?"* question is a disguise for a much deeper one:

Who are you in your work?

This is the question that begins to surface your real professional identity. It asks you to name yourself, not the role you perform or title you've been assigned, and that slight shift changes how you activate your career, advocate for your value, and what belonging looks like for you.

If we asked each other, "How do you see yourself in your work?" instead of "What do you do?" we would understand one another more clearly. We would begin recognizing not just roles but unique identities, and that recognition is the soil where career belonging grows.

To orient yourself on how you currently see yourself, how you want to be experienced by others, and how you want your worth reflected in your work, the Three Career Power Questions are designed to do exactly this. They sit at the crossroads where career fit stops and career belonging begins.

The Turning Point Between Career Fit and Career Belonging

The shift toward career belonging almost always begins the same way: tiny disruptions in your career, nagging questions about what you want to do next, a persistent feeling that something is missing but you can't put a finger on it.

Signs of readiness often appear during career transitions or moments of misalignment and struggle. For instance when you sense your career is asking more of you than a role, a title, or a resume can answer. You might find yourself wondering:

- Why isn't my career working for me?
- Why do people misinterpret my value?
- Why can't I articulate what makes me unique?
- Why doesn't my boss or client get me?
- Who am I really in my work?

These questions are symptoms not causes. They are signals that your belonging needs—across the levels of self, others, and something greater—are not being met.

This is exactly where most people go wrong: they try to fix the symptom by finding a new job, boss, or industry without understanding the career belonging cause first, which is the better starting point.

The Three Career Power Questions: Your Starting Point

When I began providing professional identity services, I noticed clients arrived with dozens of questions about their careers. However, I quickly realized I always needed to ask them the same set of questions before anything made sense.

Those became my **Three Career Power Questions (CPQs):**

1. Who are you in your work, besides your job title?
2. What does that mean?
3. What makes you feel seen, known, and valued in your work/career?

These questions are straightforward. And, they sound simple, but they're not easy. If you struggle to answer the CPQs, good. I expected that. That's why you're reading this book.

The CPQs are designed to reveal how little clarity you have around your professional identity and belonging needs. These questions are the gateway to the entire journey ahead. This is the moment where you must turn inward before your external reality can match your desires.

In Chapter 4, you learned the Three Levels of Belonging: self, others, and something greater. The Career Power Questions map directly onto that framework.

- **CPQ #1** ("Who are you in your work?") reflects your sense of belonging to *self*.
- **CPQ #2** ("What does that mean?") reveals how you want to be *understood by others*.
- **CPQ #3** ("What makes you feel seen, known, and valued?") clarifies how you want to be *reflected by others and connected to something greater than yourself*.

Together, these questions orient your current self-understanding in your career. If your self-awareness is less than you expected or realized, that's okay. You're about to embark on a journey to gain these insights.

Before moving on, there is **one** crucial requirement when answering the CPQs: **your answers must be work-focused only.**

The moment you drift into hobbies, personal qualities, life roles, or identities outside your professional life, the integrity of the questions breaks down. For example, if you answer "Who are you in your work?" with "I'm a team player, great problem solver, volunteer for local charities, marathoner, and parent," you lose the precision that makes the CPQs powerful.

While all of your identities and personality traits matter because they are part of who you are as a human, this type of response answers the "whole self" question. The "Who are you in your work?" question is specific to your work life, and we're not accustomed to naming that part of ourselves succinctly and accurately.

Answering the CPQs is hard because most people have never been asked to separate *who I am as a person* from *who I truly am in my work*. The CPQs force that distinction.

There's another constraint that matters just as much: **you must answer using identity words, not descriptors.** Identity words are nouns. They name who you are. Too often, people answer with adjectives or traits, saying things like, *"I'm innovative, thoughtful, ambitious, and really good at building relationships."* Those describe *how* you operate, not *who* you are in your work.

What I see, without exception, although the CPQs are short, memorable, and deceptively simple, **almost no one answers them well on the first try.** Not executives. Not high achievers. Not creatives, technologists, or leaders. And certainly not multi-hyphenates.

No one.

That's part of their elegant design. The CPQs are diagnostic. They reveal the exact gap this work is designed to address.

The Gap: When People Try to Answer the CPQs (and Can't)

Here's what typically happens when I ask the CPQs. Imagine I'm at a networking event meeting someone new:

> **Me:** Hi, Edward. Great to meet you, I'm Sarabeth. I see your nametag says you're a Product Director. How do you see yourself in your work, besides your job title?

> **Edward:** Well, I'm a bit of a jack-of-all-trades. I lead our product team, but I also build relationships across our network and support our innovation strategy.

Me: Really, what does that mean?

Edward: Well, it's a lot to explain. Basically, I'm a problem solver and I jump into a lot of projects.

Me: Interesting, that does sound like a lot. So, what makes you feel seen, known, and valued in your career as a jack-of-all-trades who solves a lot of problems?

Edward: Huh? I'm not sure. I've never thought about that. Probably as an innovator.

This scenario is more the norm than the exception. People are caught off guard by the question "Who are you in your work?" because they assume I'm asking, "What do you do?" So they answer with tasks, roles, or job descriptions rather than a clear professional identity.

An overwhelming number of people default to generic labels like "jack-of-all-trades" or say "I wear a lot of hats." These phrases reveal the very problem the CPQs are designed to surface: people don't actually know who they are in their work. (And, they've given up trying to explain all their hats because it takes too much effort.)

By the second question, most people slip into industry jargon or long lists of responsibilities. Their identity becomes less clear, not more. And when we reach the third question, nearly everyone falters. They either repeat a familiar cliché ("I want to be seen as a servant leader" or "I want to be known as a collaborator") or admit they've never considered the question at all. These responses aren't wrong, they're simply unexamined. They reflect the scripts we've been taught, not the truth we carry.

Now compare that to someone who *can* answer the CPQs. When people *can* answer them clearly, everything changes. I'll share another scenario:

> **Me:** Hi, Edward. Great to meet you, I'm Sarabeth. I see your nametag says you're a Product Director. How do you see yourself in your work, besides your job title?
>
> **Edward:** Great question. I am the Product Director but I see myself as the Idea Architect.
>
> **Me:** Really? How interesting. What does that mean?
>
> **Edward:** I work at the intersection of storytelling, data analysis, and client engagement to shape ideas that clients want and that my team is talented enough to build. I catalyze the best ideas from my team so we create exceptional products the market needs.

Me: Wow. That's a great description. What makes you feel seen, known, and valued in your work as an Idea Architect?

Edward: I feel seen during meetings when someone on my team leans over and gives me the dry erase marker because they know I'm about to go into *idea architect* mode and sketch all over the whiteboard. I feel most valued when clients come back two or three years later and tell me our products are still performing at a high level for them. I want to be known as someone who inspires and brings out the best ideas in a group.

You can sense the difference immediately. Edward #2 is grounded, specific, and expressive. His answers are not only clearer, they are more human. He reveals the essence of who he is in his work, which makes it easier to understand his value and connect authentically. You learn in seconds what Edward #1 never actually told you.

And here's the kicker: **Edward #1 and Edward #2 are the same person.**

The only difference is self-awareness and language. Edward #2 has access to the words that illuminate his identity and belonging needs.

Unpacking Why the Career Power Questions Work

QUESTION 1: *Who Are You in Your Work?*

This question asks you to name yourself in your work—*not the role you fill, but the identity you inhabit.* I call this your **professional identity**, which you'll explore in depth in Chapter 8. Most people instinctively answer with a job title or a generic label like entrepreneur, manager, or problem solver. But these terms describe functions, not your authentic identity.

Question one pushes you to articulate who you are at your best in your work, the throughline behind everything you touch. Examples include Opportunity Translator, Polisher of Diamonds in the Rough, Moment Architect, Breakthrough Activator, or Tension Methodologist. These labels make people lean in because they reveal something essential, novel, distinct, and true about you. Depending on the context or what you're more comfortable with, there are alternative versions of this question you can also use:

- How do you see yourself in your work?
- What title would you give yourself?

QUESTION 2: *What Does That Mean?*

"What does that mean?" is really shorthand for "Why does this matter?" Once you name who you are (especially if it's uncommon like Breakthrough Activator), you **must** define it. This is where you articulate the meaning behind your identity: how it shows up in your work, the values that shape it, and the contributions it generates for others. I often instruct people to use the phrase "I work at the intersection of X, Y, and Z" as a way of signaling their complex value.

Similar to the first question, there are a few alternative versions of this question you can try:

- How do you define your professional identity? What does it mean?
- What are you doing when you are a [insert professional identity name]?
- What does your professional identity mean to others? To the world/ market/ clients?

QUESTION 3: What Makes You Feel Seen, Known, and Valued in Your Career?

This question is the bridge between **identity** and **belonging**. It asks you to describe what recognition looks and *feels like* for you—how you want your professional identity to be mirrored by colleagues, supervisors, clients, and your broader field.

If you can't name what makes you feel seen, known, and valued, then you can't create career belonging. You will default to whatever others project onto you. In Part 2, you'll create three SKVs—your Seen, Known, and Valued statements—to be able to articulate this with precision.

Moving Forward

The CPQs are more than a set of reflective prompts. They're a tuning fork. They initiate the deeper work of uncovering your professional identity and your career belonging needs. Working on your answers allows you to see where your language flows easily and where it collapses. You notice which parts of your professional identity feel solid and which feel vague, borrowed, or flimsy. This is critical information that shows where your career belonging is absent, already present and where it's still forming.

Now you're ready to begin Part 2, a highly interactive section where you'll be guided through the Five Steps to Career Belonging. Your answers to the CPQs will be revisited along the way to help you sharpen, evolve, and deepen them and eventually reach a polished version.

Next Steps

- **Reflect**: Which of the Three Career Power Questions is easiest for you to answer right now? Which is the hardest?

- **Define**: Write a first draft/first attempt of your answer to: *Who are you in your work besides your job title?* See what happens.

- **Do**: Test out the CPQs on your colleagues and friends. Notice how well they answer on their first try and where they struggle.

ACHIEVING CAREER BELONGING

CHAPTER 6

The Five Steps to Career Belonging

"Yesterday, I was clever, so I wanted to change the world. Today I am wise, so I'm changing myself."

—Rumi

Up until now, this book has focused on the core problem: what isn't working and *why* career fit falls short. We've unpacked belonging and *what* career belonging actually is. In this section, we shift into the *how*, guided by actionable tools and prompts.

This part of the journey is reflective, and at times uncomfortable in the best possible way. You are about to question assumptions about your career that you've carried for years, develop a deeper relationship with your professional identity, and learn how to actively create the conditions to achieve career belonging.

I know from years of experience that this work will change how you see yourself and your career. It will force you to slow down, to notice things you've learned to ignore, and to question stories you've been telling yourself for a very long time.

By the time you reach the end of the five steps, you will have:

- a clearer sense of who you are in your work
- language for why career belonging matters to you
- and a framework to articulate how you want to be seen, known, and valued on your terms

To describe what this transformation feels like, I want to share a metaphor from artist, designer, and photographer Dario Calmese, a deeply hybrid professional, who once reflected on how learning something true can rearrange your entire inner world:

> Any information we learn, we're walking through life with certain paradigms in place. Kind of like a room. When something new is introduced, either you rearrange everything to make space for it or you reject it so that everything stays the same. The easy thing to do is just to reject the new and let everything stay the same,

but that was an undeniable thing [for me].
To let that in, everything had to change,
and everything came into question.

As you move through the next chapters, I invite you to let your definition of "career" become an opportunity to question everything. Some beliefs will need rearranging. Others will need to be tossed out or even wholly remodeled. That is the undeniable point of this section.

How the Five Steps Work

Career belonging doesn't happen by accident, and it doesn't happen all at once. It's something you build, through reflection, language, and action. The five steps are intentionally sequenced. They're designed to awaken you, reconnect you with your sense of self, and rekindle a deeper sense of self-awareness about who you are and how your career belongs to you. I invite you to explore each step with curiosity, openness, and delight.

One important note before we begin: Step Four, the Career Belonging Matrix, is the peak experience of the process. It's the keystone you're building toward—the moment where everything you've been uncovering comes together and starts to make sense in a more integrated way. It's truly a one-of-a-kind tool I hope you will use again and again across your careerspan.

Here's the overview of where you're headed:

Step One: Assess Your State of Career Being and Career Persona. We begin by getting honest about where you are in your career. This step helps you identify your current state of career being and the persona you've been operating from, often without realizing it. It creates a baseline from which to move forward.

Step Two: Clarify Your Authentic Professional Identity. This is where many people have their first real breakthrough. You'll begin naming who you are in your work beyond your job title. You'll explore whether your identity is singular, multiple, or hybrid, and start articulating the essence of how you operate professionally. This step gives you language you may have been missing for years. It's also where you'll answer the first two Career Power Questions: *Who are you in your work? And, what does that mean?*

Step Three: Define Your Big C Career versus Little c Career. Here's where the confusion starts to untangle. Most people spend their lives chasing a little c career, the one shaped by expectations, ladders, and external validation. In this step, you'll clarify what your Big C Career is, the one that reflects your agency, values, and deeper sense of direction. This distinction alone changes how you make decisions.

Step Four: Complete the Career Belonging Matrix. This is where everything comes together. The Career Belonging Matrix helps you integrate what you've learned across the three levels of belonging: self, others, and something greater. It turns insight into structure and gives you a clear picture of what career belonging actually looks like for *you*. This is the hallmark framework for career reflection.

Step Five: Become Seen, Known, and Valued. Finally, you translate reflection into language. You'll create a master set of Seen, Known, and Valued statements that articulate how you want to experience belonging in your career. These statements become anchors for communication, boundaries, and choice-making. They help you stop hoping others will "get you" and start expressing what matters directly. This is when you answer the third career power question: *What makes you feel seen, known, and valued in your work/career?*

These five steps work together, and when taken in sequence, they create a shift that's internal and visible.

A Note on Pace (and Permission)

I want to normalize something before you begin. This work can feel mentally and emotionally demanding. The most common feedback I receive is people say this is the deepest career reflection they've ever done. That's not because it's complicated. It's because we're rarely asked to think this carefully about who we are in our work.

Feeling confused, resistant, or temporarily uncertain is perfectly normal. It means you're thinking in new ways. Meta-reflection, thinking about how you think and who you are, takes energy. This is gentle foreshadowing of what to expect, but also a testimonial of the power of this process.

Jobs, Careers, and Why Belonging Is Different

One more thing before moving forward, it's important to clarify that career belonging is not about finding a job, a career, or even a calling. Psychologists Amy Wrzesniewski and Jane Dutton describe three orientations we have toward our work. We see it as either a job, a career, or a calling. In their definition, a job pays the bills, a career focuses on advancement, and a calling brings meaning.

Career belonging can exist alongside any of these. You don't need to know your calling. You don't need to abandon a practical job or shift your ambition. What you *do* need is alignment between who you are and how your work reflects that. That's what these five steps are designed to help you connect.

Looking Ahead

In the next chapter, you'll begin Step One where you'll assess your current state of career being and the career persona that shapes how you approach your career. Are you stuck? Disconnected? Restless? Lost in transition? Burned out? Going through a reinvention? Each of these represents a different state of being, and it shapes how you experience your career and what actions will actually support you.

Knowing the exact state you're in reveals a critical insight: *how you uniquely move through your career* and *what works for you specifically.* This is your baseline as you journey towards career belonging.

In my work, there is no one-size-fits-all career advice. Although I give a detailed overview of the states of career being and career personas, you can use an interactive AI Companion designed for this book for a more personalized experience. Find it at morethanmytitle.com.

Next Steps

- **Reflect**: Which of the five steps feels most alive or urgent for you right now?

- **Define**: Notice one curiosity or question that's coming up for you before you begin the five steps.

- **Do**: Commit to moving through the steps in order, even when it feels uncomfortable or unfamiliar.

CHAPTER 7

Step One: Assess Your State of Career Being and Career Persona

"To exist is to change; to change is to mature; to mature is to create oneself endlessly."

—*Henri Bergson*

Each of us has a distinct way of moving through the world. How you make decisions, set goals, respond to uncertainty, and take action reflects your own unique strategy, whether you know it or not.

The same is true of your career.

How you approach your work, job opportunities, and career growth follows patterns shaped by your psychological and emotional states, lived experiences, nervous system responses, and deeply ingrained habits. Understanding those patterns is essential if you want to move toward career belonging rather than default to career fit.

That's why Step One is about **understanding your orientation to your career.** Before you can evolve your career, you must know:

- the **state** you're in, and
- the **persona** through which you navigate the work world.

Offering advice, especially to yourself, without this awareness is like redesigning a house without knowing who lives there. It's a bad idea. Some people are adventurous and can't wait to pivot into a new field, whereas others are more discerning and want to test waters before committing to a change. Each type of orientation requires their own type of guidance.

Rethinking the "Career Path" You're On

Most of us were taught to think about careers in binary terms: You're either *on a path* or *off one.* If you're not on a path, then you're typically seen as:

- lost
- in limbo
- in transition
- reinventing yourself
- or figuring it out

But these labels hardly scratch the surface of what's happening. They're inadequate labels. Instead of asking, *"What career path are you on?"* I invite you to ask:

"What state of *career being* are you in?"

Pause and notice how that question lands for you. It can be emotional. Physiological. Spiritual. You should feel a reaction in your body. That's because you are always in *some* state of career being, even when you're not on a path. Knowing your current state of career being establishes your current orientation and outlook on your career.

So, What If You're "In-Between" Paths?

During one of my most intense periods of career liminality, I felt consumed by one question: *How do I get unstuck?* One day, while doomscrolling on my phone, I came across a viral video by performance artist Yoann Bourgeois that completely transformed my perspective.

In the video, with graceful, almost playful movements, Yoann climbs a large freestanding staircase in a public plaza. Every few steps, he deliberately falls off the staircase onto a trampoline below, bouncing once or twice before rebounding, getting back on the staircase, climbing a few more stairs and falling off again and again, until he finally reaches the top. Even at the top, he falls off a few more times and casually rebounds. It was mesmerizing to watch.

(Scan to watch Yoann Bourgeois's performance on the trampoline.)

For me, the performance wasn't about falling and getting back up again, which would have been the obvious takeaway. Instead, it was about the airbound moments. When Yoann was suspended mid-fall or mid-rebound, touching nothing, he was calm, almost serene. He wasn't fighting gravity. He wasn't bracing for impact. He just was. Being in the air mattered as much to the performance as the concrete steps he took.

That's when I had my epiphany: **Careers aren't defined by being on or off a path. They exist in multiple states, and these invisible states deserve their own names.**

Yoann's performance contained three states:

1. the stairs
2. the trampoline
3. and the space in between them

That in-between space is the most potent and hard to describe. It's the one we often fear, try to avoid, rush through or escape from, but it's an essential space, and you can choose how you react when you're in it.

How you navigate and behave in the in-between says a lot about you. It reveals your stress response as well as your ability (or inability) to move away from or toward what you truly want. Whenever we pathfind, we move between and through other states along the way. That's a crucial component of the career belonging journey. Let's name these additional states.

The Nine States of Career Being

Yoann's performance led me to identify **nine distinct states of career being**, which are ways people actually experience their careers, especially under stress, transition, or change.

Instead of viewing your career as merely a series of high points, low points, or transition points, consider the in-between spaces and how you felt in them. Did you stay rigid on the steps for fear of jumping? Did you combat the fall, making the landing rough? Did you scream and complain, cursing the world as gravity pulled you down? Or did you embrace weightlessness and laugh on the way up and on the way down? These are merely a few possibilities, but you can start to imagine yourself and reflect on how you've handled these moments in the past.

The nine states of career being are not linear or permanent. Many are linked to trauma and stress responses because careers are one of the primary arenas where fear, identity, safety, and worth collide, which triggers stress.

The following nine states of being are meant to be descriptive labels for how careers feel:

1. Career Pathing
2. Career Pathlessness
3. Career Fight
4. Career Fright
5. Career Freeze
6. Career Fawning
7. Career Flight
8. Career Fit
9. Career Belonging

Your goal right now is to identify:

- the state you're in now
- and how you actually feel in that state

I'll share a short description about each of the nine states of career being:

Career Pathing is perhaps the most familiar state. Being on a career path is an ideal state for people who thrive with a clear trajectory, marked by recognizable milestones and goalposts. Career pathing is a recognized term in career and professional development, and this state is comforting to many because it provides direction and purpose. However, being on a career path doesn't mean that everything is smooth sailing. Even when you're on a path, you may question whether it's the right one, or if it will lead you where you want to be. The challenge in this state is to remain flexible and open to change.

Career Pathlessness is characterized by uncertainty, confusion, and a lack of direction. You may feel lost, unsure of what you want, or unable to see a path forward. This state can be disorienting and frustrating, especially when society often pressures us to be on a defined path. Career pathlessness can be triggered by a career setback or a desire for change. The challenge here is to accept that it's okay to be pathless. This state can be an opportunity for deep reflection and exploration.

Career Fight is a state where you feel the need to push back or struggle against obstacles in your career. This might involve fighting to regain a lost position, battling a toxic work environment, or struggling within yourself to stay motivated. While this state can be exhausting, it also builds resilience. The challenge is to know when to keep fighting and when to let go. Sometimes the best choice is to change direction. Career fight is a state of resistance and perseverance, not endurance.

Career Fright is when fear dominates your professional life. This state often arises after a negative experience, such as a job loss, failure, or harsh criticism that shakes your confidence. You might find yourself afraid to take risks, apply for new roles, or even speak up in meetings.

Career fright can be paralyzing, holding you back from pursuing your goals. The challenge is rebuilding your confidence and learning to trust yourself again. It's about facing your fears and taking small steps forward. Career fright needs safety before strategy.

Career Freeze is a state of stagnation. You feel stuck, unable to move forward or make progress in your career. This might happen if you're in a job that no longer challenges you, or if you're unemployed and can't seem to find a new opportunity. Career freeze is marked by inaction, whether caused by indecision, fear, or external circumstances. It might involve taking small steps, such as networking, upskilling, or applying for jobs outside your comfort zone. The challenge is to start moving, even if it's in a direction you hadn't initially considered. Breaking out of career freeze requires momentum.

Career Fawning is a state of pleasing or appeasing the needs of others. You might be having a hard time saying "no," pretending to agree when you really don't, and doing what you're told to do in your career regardless of what you think. It's similar to career freeze because you're staying put rather than running away or fighting back. Ultimately, by putting the needs of others before your own, your needs aren't being met. The challenge is becoming more self-aware and setting boundaries so you can begin to prioritize yourself.

Career Flight is the state of running away from your career. This might happen when you feel overwhelmed, unfulfilled, or simply desperate for a change. In career flight, you might leave a job abruptly, change industries, or even take a break from your career altogether. The challenge is while career flight may be a necessary escape from a toxic or unfulfilling situation, it's essential to ensure you're not just running away as a reaction. It should be a strategic move.

Career Fit is the state of aligning your skills, qualifications, and experiences with the demands of a job or role. It often brings stability and validation. In this state, you are focused on meeting expectations, ensuring you are the "right fit" for the position or organization. However, this state can feel limiting if it requires you to suppress parts of your authentic self to conform. The challenge is to recognize when it no longer serves your deeper needs. That's when it might be time to move beyond simply fitting in to finding true belonging in your work.

Finally, there's **Career Belonging**. In this state, you're no longer attached to external measures of success or fitting a mold. Wherever you are is where you choose to be. You feel aligned with your work. You can earn a solid living, work for a company or work for yourself and be in a state of career belonging. The challenge is career belonging requires deep self-reflection, self-esteem and self-awareness, the courage to follow your unique career direction and often design it yourself, and the perseverance to question and break away from convention.

Now that we've covered the nine states of career being, which one resonates most with you?

You may experience one state at a time or a combination. The duration of time you stay in a state could be months to years. The states correspond with your personal development, psychological well being, sense of self, and life and career situation. Only you can determine which state you're in and when you've shifted into a new one.

The Eleven Career Personas

If the nine states tell us **where you are in your career**, then the career personas tell us **how you like to move through it**. The two go together to create a complete picture of your approach.

No matter what state of career being you're in, you approach it through a particular lens: a habitual way of interpreting risk, opportunity, and direction. How do you decide when to go left or right, forward or backward, or stay put? How are you perceiving opportunities versus threats? That lens, that inner guidance that's helping you know what to do, is what informs your **career persona**.

Personas are not roles or traits. They are *styles*. Any state can pair with any persona. This is what creates your special nuance and why career advice must be customized to meet you where you are.

Below are the career personas. Choose which one sounds most like you:

The Path Follower prefers a traditional, goal-oriented approach. You like to follow a beaten path or walk in the footsteps of others, moving from point A to Z in a structured way.

The Bushwhacker pursues rough, overgrown terrain, forging their own way. You're doing your own thing, and you're comfortable with uncertainty and exploration.

The Trailblazer carves a new trail that no one has been on before. Part innovator and part disruptor. You're determined, driven, and ready to overcome obstacles to create something original.

The Forager makes do with what they find, seeing every opportunity as a chance to learn and grow. You're resourceful, scrappy, and always looking for ways to turn challenges into opportunities.

The Criss-Crosser moves between multiple paths, revisiting old ones and exploring new ones. You're comfortable with change and enjoy the variety that comes from trying different things.

The Nomad or Wanderer sets off without a clear agenda, allowing things to unfold naturally. You're invigorated by new experiences and find your sense of place wherever you are.

The Groundskeeper or Steward finds one path or one part of a path that they love and stays there, tending to it and helping others along the way. You're committed to maintaining and improving your chosen spot.

The Pilot prefers to see the big picture from 30,000 feet, moving as the crow flies, rather than being confined by roads and geography. You watch the horizon line, see turbulence ahead, and focus on how to arrive safely at the destination.

The Caretaker holds space for others as they pursue their paths and often serves as the glue in teams or systems. Your strength is in connection, cohesion, and emotional wellbeing.

The Seeker is guided by an inner quest instead of the external world. You're less concerned with titles or status and more devoted to finding purpose, truth, and self-alignment as your journey.

The Hybrid is a blend of any of the above personas. You're a combination that fluctuates based on your needs and goals.

Imagine how the personas and states play together. A bushwhacker in a state of career fight is likely spending enormous energy fighting systems and hacking through their career jungle, trying to make their way against seemingly impossible odds. A criss-crosser in career fit might be worried about changing jobs again and what damage that might cause their reputation. Or, a groundskeeper in career flight is fleeing from a place where they've been rooted for a long time, and they feel immense loss and dislocation.

Each persona requires different support, even if they're in the same state of career being. That's why this language is invaluable for helping assess and express what's really happening in your career.

How This All Fits Together

If we reduce the states and personas into a math equation, it would be:

**Your State of Career Being +
Your Career Persona =
How You're Currently Approaching Your Career**

This equation is not *who* you are. It's how you're operating in your career *right now*. Once you can name that, everything else becomes easier to work with.

I didn't have this language until my forties. I didn't know why I felt anxious, unsafe, or frozen in roles that looked "good on paper." In reality, I was moving through career fawning and career freeze while embodying personas, like the trailblazer, that required risk and visibility. I didn't feel safe to be my true self in roles. I was worried about being seen as too much or being managed out. And, after being laid off twice in two years, I became painfully stuck in career fright.

Without this language, I blamed myself for poorly handling my transitions. Feeling guilty, complaining to friends and having low self-worth. With this language, I understood what I was personally dealing with and up against. This matters more than people realize. This terminology helps us represent what is happening inside ourselves, rather than defaulting to expressions like, "I don't think this role is a good fit for me," or "I'm lost right now." There is so much more to it than that.

These terms serve as a new set of vocabulary to shift how we collectively think and talk about our careers at a societal level. When you can name your state of career being and recognize your career persona, you stop pathologizing yourself and start understanding your patterns.

Knowing *how* you approach your career helps you express your unique needs so you get the right support. The next layer is knowing *who* you are in it, shifting from orientation to identification. In the next chapter, you'll begin clarifying your authentic professional identity, separating who you are in your work from the roles you've performed, the expectations you've inherited, and the labels you've been given.

This is where your career starts becoming something that belongs to you.

Next Steps

- **Reflect:** What state of career being are you currently in?

- **Define:** Which career persona feels most familiar to you right now?

- **Do:** Journal one small change that could help you move toward career belonging. And, if you'd like more support, scan the QR code in this chapter for AI-enabled guidance.

(Scan this code to explore your current state of career being and career persona through an AI-powered reflection tool.)

CHAPTER 8

Step Two: Clarify Your Authentic Professional Identity

"What if our habitual idea of who we are is nothing more than that—habits of thinking, remembering, imagining? What if just for an instant, those thoughts of 'me' ceased? Who are we then?"

—Henry Shukman

You can't be seen, known, and valued for something you haven't named or can't easily communicate. That's why career belonging requires identity clarity. These two go hand in hand.

First and foremost, your professional identity is not your job title. Research shows that job loss can, and often does, trigger an identity crisis. Most people don't realize how tightly they've welded their sense of self to a job title, until it disappears.

A job title can be taken away from you. It can be changed overnight. You can outgrow it. You can lose it. But your professional identity is something you "have" because you embody it, it belongs to you.

Job titles are useful. They're also wildly inadequate and not going anywhere anytime soon. They're socially imposed labels designed by workforce systems to sort and create org charts, compensation systems, and leveling frameworks. They classify you for benefits and structure, but they rarely capture the full scope of how you operate, what you bring, or what you're actually known for when you're at your best. That's what your professional identity is about.

Definition of Professional Identity

Your professional identity is a noun. I like to say it's **how you see yourself in your work** or **it's what you choose to call yourself**.

When people don't "get" you, when they misunderstand your role, misread your value, or try to pigeonhole you, it's often because your professional identity is undefined, unexpressed, or overshadowed by language that's too generic for you.

Your professional identity is what you call yourself besides your job title. That last part matters. This is not about your whole self. This isn't "I'm a mom," "I'm a runner," "I'm a friend," or "I'm an introvert." Those identities can be real, important truths about who you are, but they're not what we're defining here.

Your professional identity consists of your values, beliefs, ethics, talents, behaviors, and skills *in your work*. It's especially evident in what appears most consistently when you're in your zone of genius at work.

Your job title might be Product Manager, but your professional identity might be Empathetic Storyteller. Your job title might be Founder, but your professional identity might be Wildest Dream Director. Your job title might be Events Coordinator, but your professional identity might be Moment Architect. You get the picture.

Author James Clear says, "Every action you take is a vote for the type of person you wish to become. No single instance will transform your beliefs, but as the votes build up, so does the evidence of your new identity." I love this because it tells us where identity comes from. It's not in what we claim about ourselves, but in how we live our work.

As I've said, your professional identity is who *you* say you are, and who you want to be seen, known, and valued as.

Study Your Identity In Action

When someone asks me, "How do I figure out who I am in my work?" I tell them to study the ways they do their work to see their identity in action. While it's not easy for us to see ourselves, we can examine our actions to give us strong clues.

Try it for yourself. Study the way you do your work, especially the things you take for granted or that nobody else does quite as well as you do. Let's say you're the best at making slide decks. Notice the way you make them. How do you start? Track every little step, every mouse click, every sticky note you write to yourself. Do you draw your own custom illustrations? Do you gather stats from a certain source? Do you have a special way of critiquing your layouts before sharing it with colleagues? Every detail in your process matters. You may not realize it, but your identity is there, hiding in tiny moments. And each moment is a clue to your greater professional identity.

Here's an example from my own life. If you watched our nanny with our son for ten minutes, you'd immediately see she's more than a child care worker. She anticipates his needs before he can express them. She interprets his babbles like fluent language. She responds to the emotional subtext, not just his behavior.

While "nanny" is her job title, her professional identity is closer to Child Whisperer. That's a significant difference in language. One label collapses her into a role, and the other reveals her authentic self.

The difference between being seen as a job title and being seen for your professional identity is the difference between being labeled as a role and being *recognized* for your uniqueness. Your professional identity makes your unique value more visible.

The Sweet Spot: Distinct But Not Confusing

A strong professional identity hits a special sweet spot. It helps you stand out while still being understandable. Sociologist Marilyn Brewer calls this balance optimal distinctiveness, the human need to belong *and* to be unique at the same time.

What this means is if you're too generic, your professional identity disappears into a sea of sameness (how many leaders or problem solvers have you met? Probably hundreds). If you're too abstract, people can't place you or grasp when to involve you (What would you hire a person for who calls themself the Master of Internal Synergies? It's too outlandish). You're looking for the sweet spot that's both novel and relatable.

My optimal distinctiveness is being a Creative Disruptor because I work at the intersection of being an artist, educator, designer, and researcher. As a Creative Disruptor, I reimagine what's possible and test unconventional ideas to create positive change.

This identity has become my career compass. It expresses what I'm for, what I'm not for, what conditions I need to thrive, and what kinds of opportunities I should stop saying yes to, even if they look good on paper. Over time, this is how a professional identity becomes your personal brand.

Your professional identity cascades into your presence, how others reference and remember you, and it becomes what you're known for, besides your previous job titles and work history. This is why your professional identity is durable and critical to building your personal brand.

Professional Identity Is Not Personal Branding

There's a big difference between identity and branding. People often jump straight to personal branding as a solution when they're trying to become more visible in their work. But they don't realize that branding without professional identity clarity is empty and often meaningless. It becomes a cliche or collection of buzzwords and borrowed positioning.

Your personal brand is **how you *intentionally put* your professional identity into the world.** Companies do this all the time, and they do it strategically. First, they define who they are and come up with a name for their company before they design how their brand looks and feels. They spend weeks developing a brand identity to reflect their sweet spot in the market, and then visual branding, a logo and messaging follows.

Same for you. Your professional identity must be uncovered before your personal brand can be built. And, your professional identity gets clearer over time as you evolve in your own understanding of yourself and your career. In your early years, you might have some sense of who you are, but you learn more about yourself as you gain more life and work experience. Hindsight allows you to see the common thread that weaves your constellation of work experiences together (notice I did not use the word jobs).

Discover Your Type of Professional Identity

Career frameworks tend to reduce professionals into one of two categories, "experts or generalists." There are longstanding debates on the value of each. But, in my book *More Than My Title*, I argue there are three types of professional identity because professionals aren't binary, especially these days.

Decide which type resonates with you most after reviewing each description.

THREE TYPES OF PROFESSIONAL IDENTITY

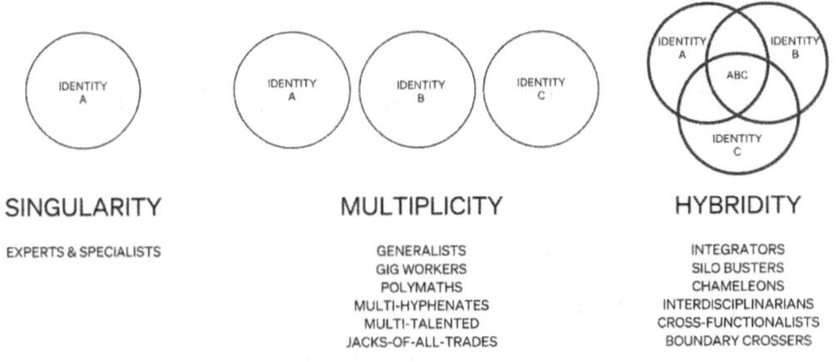

Singularity: The Expert or Specialist

Singularity is the most straightforward. People with singularity tend to experience their work identity through one primary profession or role. They say, "I'm a dermatologist," "I'm a civil engineer," or "I'm a litigator." Their career belonging is often tied to mastery and depth. They like staying in one lane and becoming the go-to person.

The risk of singularity is not that it's "too narrow." The risk is what happens when the lane shifts, when the market changes, the role becomes obsolete, or life forces a reinvention. Individuals with singularity may struggle to redefine themselves. To maintain career belonging, they must focus on continuous learning and remain open to evolving within their chosen field.

Multiplicity: The Generalist or Multi-Talented Professional

Multiplicity is not a lack of focus. It's a *plural identity*. This category has a thousand names: generalist, jack-of-all-trades, multi-hyphenate, multipotentialite, polymath, Renaissance person. If it starts with "multi," it's probably pointing at this type.

People with multiplicity have multiple professional identities that coexist side-by-side:

- "I'm a consultant, a writer, and an educator."
- "I'm a designer and a coach."
- "I'm a marketer and a community builder."

They find fulfillment in having a diversity of work projects, whether self-employed or working for an employer.

The challenge with multiplicity is usually curation, coherence, and communication. When someone asks,

"What do you do?" the answer can sound like a list. And lists invite misunderstanding, skepticism, or under-valuation, especially in environments obsessed with categorization.

Hybridity: The Category Defier

Hybridity is the most complex of the three types of identity, and it's where a lot of people feel alone. Hybrids don't just have multiple professional identities. They *integrate* them to create something new and work at the intersection of their identities, like a Venn diagram. That's why employers struggle to understand their full value. Hybridity doesn't fit neatly into one box.

The MIT professor, Neri Oxman, is a classic example of a hybrid. She's an architect, scientist, designer, and artist combined. She defies categorization because she has hybridized into something that doesn't exist inside one academic department or field. Her hybridity has led her to be the pioneer of material ecology, which is a groundbreaking methodology across art, engineering, and science.

Hybrids tend to be translators, integrators, boundary crossers, and bridge builders. They create value as the connective tissue between teams, disciplines, systems, and problems. While their value can be hard to discern and measure, it's often seen in the quality and amount of diversity of thought and radical relationships they bring together.

Creative director, photographer, and design theorist Dario Calmese captures his hybridity beautifully when he describes it this way:

> [It's like] me saying the same thing in different languages. Each medium allows for a certain type of communication, weaving together seemingly disparate ideas and sharing them with somebody else so they can follow along with your thought process.

The ArtLab at Harvard says Dario works at the nexus of art, fashion, and academia, and he uses his "knowledge of movement, gesture, and psychology to create complex characters and narratives that explore history, race, class, and what it means to be human."

For me, I didn't have language for my hybridity until my late thirties. I just knew I felt most alive when my work allowed me to integrate my primary professional identities, which are: artist, educator, researcher, and designer. Roles where I've thrived allowed me to integrate these four identities in a meaningful way. But, when a role didn't allow me to, I felt off-center and I shrank. I replaced myself with a version I thought would be easier for others to understand and accept, which is why I eventually left those roles. I felt too confined.

Today, my career belonging is when I don't have to squeeze myself into something or reduce myself. I get to be my full professional self in my work, and I'm valued for it.

Define Your Professional Identity

Once you know whether you're singular, multiple, or hybrid, you can own it and stop trying to be a structure that you're not. The goal isn't just to know your professional identity type, the goal is to clarify how many professional identities you need to name in order to be your authentic self in your work.

Important note: not all professional identities are equal. You have primary professional identities (the ones you use the most, that energize you, you want to be known for, and that reflect your deepest areas of expertise), and you have secondary ones (important, but not as central), and you can have tertiary identities and so forth. You must know your primary ones because those are the identities you lead with, while your other identities are drawn upon as needed.

As a general guide:

- **Singularity:** define one primary professional identity
- **Multiplicity:** define 2–3 primary professional identities (otherwise your list gets too long)

- **Hybridity:** define 2–4 primary professional identities, then craft the "intersection name" that captures who you are when they all overlap

  (SIDENOTE: In hybridity, things get trickier because you're hybridizing multiple identities together. I bet you're wondering how you introduce yourself and talk about your hybridity. I've developed a comprehensive process to help jacks-of-all-trades and hybrid professionals identify and brand themselves. It starts with the phrase "I work at the intersection of X, Y, and Z," with XYZ representing your primary professional identities. Check out my website for more resources to explore the intersection of your multiple professional identities and craft a name that captures the essence of who you are in that space.)

Regardless of whether you're singular, multiple, or hybrid, the following steps will help you brainstorm your professional identities and determine which ones are your primary.

Step 1: Create a Professional Identity Inventory

List every professional identity you've ever been in your work. Go beyond your resume. Include how you operate, not just what you've been paid to do. Start by considering the roles and identities you embody in your daily work.

You might list words like: advocate, challenger, synthesizer, builder, translator, mentor.

If you get stuck, start with "I am…" statements, but keep them work-centered like: "I am a leader," "I am a brainstormer," "I am an opportunity finder," or "I am an empath."

Remember, identities are nouns, declarations of who you are in your work and how you see yourself. They are not verbs or descriptions like "I am kind," "I am generous," or "I am smart." Those are traits. If you write, "I am thoughtful" to describe yourself in your work, translate it into a professional identity, which might be "I am a sensemaker."

Step 2: Expand Your List

Challenge yourself to come up with at least fifty different professional identities. Yes, fifty. This is because the first ten will be super obvious. The next ten will start to get your juices flowing, and the next thirty will deliver slices of creative gold. This is how you outgrow generic answers.

Don't settle for terms like "problem solver" or "collaborator" or "relationship builder." Those are professional wallpaper or as I like to say vanilla terms. If you're going to do this, stretch your sense of yourself. Metaphors count. Short phrases count. "Orchestra conductor" counts. "Three-ring circus leader" counts. (Sometimes those are closer to the truth than corporate nouns.)

This can feel daunting, but it's a critical part of the process.

This step isn't about accuracy, it's about range and expansion. The more identities you list, the deeper you dig into who you truly are in your work. Aim for cleverness and uniqueness in your word choice. Use a thesaurus. Juxtaposition is also a powerful tool here. If you're a great problem solver, maybe you're an even better problem finder or problem extinguisher!

I promise you have more professional identities than you think.

Step 3: Narrow Down to Your Primary Professional Identities

Now it's time to shift from expansion to discernment. Take your list of fifty professional identities. You'll likely notice clusters—words that are related or synonymous. Group those together and look for the strongest expression within each theme. This refinement step helps surface the identities that carry the most signal.

Read your list out loud and pay attention to how each one lands in your body. Which ones energize you? Which ones feel like relief? Which ones feel funny? Which ones are your truth? This is not a purely cognitive exercise. It's somatic. Your body knows before your brain does. So check in with how each word feels in your body.

When you're ready to narrow, pay attention to the identities that:

- feel the most true
- reflect your greatest areas of expertise
- are how you want to be known
- register clearly in your body, not just your head
- And, by the way, one primary professional identity can be aspirational but the rest should reflect how you see yourself today

Whenever you are uncertain about an identity, say the phrase "I am a [identity word]" a few times out loud. I know it sounds funny, but I promise it works. Sound matters. Words have vibration. Your body will respond before your mind does. Some words will fall flat. Others will feel unmistakably yours.

And, another simple way to narrow your list is to rate each identity by your confidence level from 0 to 100% confident. Any word that lands at 75% or higher is a strong candidate for a primary professional identity.

Lastly, my favorite tip of all, don't be afraid to invent language. Invention matters more than convention. How do you think I came up with the term Creative Disruptor for myself?

Step 4: Validate Your Primary Professional Identities

Your primary professional identities are the ones you consistently embody in your work—the throughline across roles, titles, and contexts. Naming them is often a moment of reinforcing who you are beyond a job title.

Validate your final list of identities through a quick activity. An identity qualifies as *primary* if it resonates across **at least three of the four dimensions below**:

- **Internal:** This identity reflects how I see myself in my work.
- **External:** This identity reflects how others experience me in my work.
- **Conscious:** This identity reflects who I am in my greatest area of expertise.
- **Unconscious:** This identity reflects who I am when I'm in flow—at ease, absorbed, and losing track of time.

When an identity tracks across at least three dimensions, it's solid and durable. It should be a strong gut "yes" and testament of you.

Again, if your professional identity is singular, you'll have one primary professional identity, if it's multiple, you'll have two to three, and if it's hybrid, you'll have two to four to validate.

This process isn't about speed, it's about honesty and attunement with yourself. You may need to sit with a few options, test them in conversation, or let them marinate over a few days. That's normal, and it happens all the time. Breakthroughs often come after pauses, not pressure.

You don't need to feel 100% certainty by the end of this step, but you do want to be about 90% certain about your professional identity before moving forward. Your career belonging will be built on these primary professional identities because they remain your backbone across roles and jobs, only shifting slightly every five or ten years, so a strong foundation matters.

(NOTE: If you're a hybrid, there's one additional step. You'll draw a Venn diagram and place your primary professional identities in each circle to examine who you are at the intersection of them. It's a bit like solving this equation: A + B + C = ABC. Then, you'll need to recall concrete examples from your work history when you experienced your multiple professional identities activated simultaneously. This is big introspective work because it's largely unconscious. If you can hone into very specific micro-moments where you were the first, best, or only at something, that is the biggest clue. From there, themes and patterns will emerge across these memories, and your hybridity will surface.)

Step 5: Define What Your Professional Identity Means

Your professional identity needs to make sense to yourself and to others, so you need to draft a definition statement. You don't need a paragraph. You just need something short and sweet you can say in ten seconds.

A simple structure is:

"I'm a [professional identity/ies], which
means I [what you do / why you do it] so
that [what result or impact you create]."

Whether you identify with a singular professional identity (like *Biomechanic*), multiple professional identities (like *Strategist, Pioneer, and Chef*), or a hybrid identity that integrates several domains (like *Opportunity Translator*), the challenge is the same: articulating the meaning of who you are in your work in a concise way so others understand who you are too.

You can always elaborate on your definition later. In fact, you should. But when you're meeting someone for the first time, introducing yourself in a new context, or trying to anchor your own sense of direction, you only have a few seconds to capture attention and spark intrigue. The clearer you are in that first impression, the more memorable you become, both to others and to yourself.

The purpose of all these steps is that your professional identity and your meaning statement are reference points. You'll return to them as you make career decisions, evaluate opportunities, and notice when something feels off. They keep you oriented to who you are as roles, titles, and work contexts change.

From Identity to Career Belonging

Once you can name who you are in your work, the next question follows:

What kind of career is this identity trying to embrace?

Your career has layers, just like your identity does. And most people are unconsciously navigating the friction between them long before they have language for it. In the next chapter, I'll introduce two distinct but interconnected concepts: your little c career and your big C Career.

Understanding the difference is essential if you want to move beyond career fit and toward career belonging. Most people feel the tension intuitively. Now we're going to explore it.

Next Steps

- **Reflect**: Do you identify more with singularity, multiplicity, or hybridity in your professional identity?

- **Define**: Write down your primary professional identities that best describe who you are in your work.

- **Do**: Test new answers to Career Power Questions #1 and #2:
    - *Who are you in your work, besides your job title?*
    - *What does that mean?*

    If your answers feel easier to say, more grounded, or more precise than before, you're on the right track.

CHAPTER 9

Step Three: Define Your Big C versus Little c Career

"Every act of creation is first an act of destruction."

—Pablo Picasso

"If you spend your time chasing butterflies, they'll fly away. But if you spend your time making a beautiful garden, the butterflies will come to you."

—Denise Boomkens

Going from a job to a career to a calling is a fairly complex process. Most people experience some form of tension, misgivings, awkward unfolding, or a growing sense that something is lacking, even if they're doing everything right.

When I studied the actual way people progress, it's more like they move between a job, a little c career, a big C Career, and—sometimes—a calling. They oscillate back and forth. This is why I broke the word *career* into two layers, little c and big C.

You see, a *little c career* reflects the familiar, inherited version of a career. It's shaped by roles, titles, credentials, external expectations, and the pursuit of fit. It's the career you're evaluated on, rewarded for, and often trapped inside.

But a *big C Career*, on the other hand, is self-defined. It's about agency, expression, and contribution. It reflects who you are becoming and how you want to be seen, not just what you've done. It's the throughline beneath your roles. It's the work that feels true, energizing, and worth doing over time.

Ironically, there's even another phase that needs to be called out. People navigate a significant gap between their little c and big C careers.

I call this gap the career chasm, and it's rarely crossed in one fell swoop. I tend to imagine it as crossing the Grand Canyon. On the way from one side to the other is where people get stuck in career fight, career flight, career freeze, career fawning, or career fright. You find yourself disoriented, undervalued, restless, or unsure of how to move forward because you don't know who you are or what to do next. You question your entire career when you're in it.

I created a visual to show how these phases look together— job, little c career, career chasm, big C Career, and calling. Although oversimplified, it's a more realistic representation of what people go through.

Crossing the chasm to your big C Career isn't just about swapping a lowercase for a capital C. Think of it as a state shift. On the other side of the chasm, people report a greater sense of career belonging, even when their external circumstances are still evolving. In Part 3, we'll dive deeper into the career chasm and all the nuances of how to cross it.

In this chapter, we'll clarify what distinguishes little c from big C Careers and the role both play. You'll learn to define what your big C Career means to you so you can reach big C Career belonging.

The first question to ask is, what is your actual career anyway?

The "Actual" Career

There's the career we talk about—the one made up of roles, responsibilities, and achievements. And then there's the career we actually live. The one that involves a deeper journey that unfolds across time, identity, risk, meaning, and change. This distinction is fundamental to career belonging.

Poet Mary Oliver captures this distinction beautifully in *Long Life* when she writes:

> "And we might, in our lives, have many thresholds, many houses to walk out from and view the stars, or to turn and go back to for warmth and company. But the real one—the actual house not of beams and nails but of existence itself—is all of earth, with no door, no address separate from our oceans or stars...For the universe is full of radiant suggestion."

Oliver's "actual house" is not the structure we occupy, but the life we inhabit. In the same way, our actual careers are not defined by titles, paths, or milestones. They are shaped by how we move through the world of work, what we give, what we refuse, what we become and what we leave behind.

Your little c career is like the structure, but your big C Career is like the life inside it. Distinguishing between little c and big C Careers isn't a philosophical indulgence. It's a matter of practicality.

If Mary Oliver helps us see career as something lived rather than built, psychologist James Hollis helps explain why ignoring that deeper career creates so much distress. Hollis asks a deceptively simple question:

> "What is wanting to enter the world through you?"

This question has little to do with ambition or goals. It points instead to an inner pressure to become ourselves, to express something essential through one's life and work. When that pressure is ignored or suppressed, Hollis writes about what he calls the *unlived life*: the quiet grief and anxiety that arises when we abandon what is trying to emerge through us.

This is where many people find themselves today in their careers. On paper, their careers appear successful. Yet internally, something feels unfulfilled, muted, or stalled. They lack clarity and language for the mismatch.

This is the dilemma between little c and big C Careers.

Why the Word Career Is Carrying Too Much Weight

When I began researching how people understand the concept of a career, I kept noticing one thing. Everyone used the word career, but almost no one meant the same thing by it.

In a dictionary, the definition is clean and utilitarian. A career is "an occupation undertaken for a significant period of a person's life." But in conversation, that definition collapses almost immediately.

People don't talk about occupations. They talk about what they sacrifice, what they're enduring, what no longer fits, and the pressure to keep going. They talk about dreams, desires, momentum, guilt, pride, fear, and meaning.

One person described their career as, "the thing that keeps my family safe, but drains everything else." Another said, "I don't even know if I have a career. I just have a series of roles that don't add up to me." Someone else told me, "I feel like I'm supposed to be grateful, but I'm deeply unsettled, and I don't know why."

Stephanie Schmitz articulated the conundrum well:

> "I'm trying to divorce the idea of thinking of a career as a list of requirements. Instead of a career quelling the negative things in my life, I want it to bring something positive. What excites me? What brings a smile to my face? What enriches my life? These are the questions I'm asking now."

Her reflection wasn't about dissatisfaction with work itself. It was about a deeper mismatch between what a career was *supposed* to be and what she actually needed it to provide.

The word *career* has been asked to carry far too much. It's doing double—and often conflicting—duty. On the one hand, it stands for roles, titles, pay, and progression.

On the other, it's meant to hold identity, longing, agency, and meaning. We are using a single word to describe two fundamentally different experiences of work, and then we wonder why guidance systems, career tools, workforce structures, conversations, and expectations keep breaking down.

That's when I realized, if we want to talk honestly about careers today, we need to separate what has been conflated for far too long.

That separation is what I call your little c career and your big C Career. They are distinct, and they deserve different attention.

Little c careers

Most of us begin our understanding of a little c career without ever thinking about it. We absorb it from parents, schools, employers, and cultural narratives about success. The little c tells us what counts, what progresses, and what is rewarded. It teaches us how to be part of the workforce.

In a little c career, momentum matters. Titles matter. Stability matters. You learn how to optimize for fit—how to match yourself with existing roles, expectations, and systems. This can feel stabilizing, in early stages. It offers structure, income, and a sense of legitimacy. Especially in the beginning, it can be exactly what you need.

Importantly, **little c careers are necessary**. They are functional and many people spend long stretches of their lives inside them. Sometimes, that is the most aligned choice. The trouble is when a little c career becomes the *only* way a person understands their working life.

Because over time, people change. Their identities evolve. Their values sharpen. Their sense of contribution deepens. But the roles available to them don't always change at the same pace. When that happens, little c careers start to feel constricting rather than supportive.

This is often when people describe feeling "stuck." They may still be performing well. They may still be advancing. But internally, something feels off.

One participant put it this way:

> "I feel like my career keeps asking me to become smaller so I can keep moving forward."

Another said:

> "I've done everything right. I just don't recognize myself in it anymore."

These are signs and signals of outgrowing a little c career. Most notably the **misalignment between your identity and how work structures value you** grows bigger and more pronounced.

When people remain in a little c career long after it no longer reflects who they are, they often cycle through familiar patterns: pushing harder to regain motivation, fantasizing about escape, freezing in indecision, or contorting themselves to meet expectations that no longer fit. This is why career fight, flight, freeze, fawning, or fright emerge.

The problem isn't the little c career. It's that the complexity of the person has evolved more than a little c career can support. Something must change.

Big C Careers

If little c careers are shaped primarily by external conditions, big C Careers are shaped primarily from the inside out. A big C Career is not about rejecting systems and structures. It's about self-authorship. It asks a different set of questions:

- Who am I and who am I becoming through my work?
- What feels meaningful for me to express in my work?
- How do I want my work to relate to my life, not compete with it?

Big C Careers are internally anchored. They are values-based, identity-led, and responsive to change. They don't require a single role, a single organization, or even a single direction. They can be singular, multiple, or hybrid. What defines them is not a rigid form, but coherence, like a constellation made up of seemingly disparate stars.

Big C Careers often feel hard to articulate. They don't show up neatly on resumes. They're not always rewarded immediately. They require discernment, trust, and integrity to stick to your guns and inner knowing. They require a willingness to listen to yourself rather than the noise around you.

Onyi Okechukwu noticed this when she reflected on her career. She told me:

> "I see that if I'm really going to find career belonging, then [my work] should feel easy for me to provide it to the world."

She described her big C Career not in terms of position or prestige, but in terms of contribution—what felt natural for her to offer and meaningful to give. That shift didn't eliminate practical concerns, like making money, but it reframed how she evaluated opportunities.

Radhika Rao experienced something similar. For years, she identified primarily as a theater artist and educator. But when she stepped back and looked across her life, another throughline became visible: peacebuilding. Theater and education weren't the point; they were expressions. Naming that changed how she understood both her past choices and her future direction.

Big C Careers often reveal themselves retroactively before they become intentional. You see it in your patterns. In what keeps returning. In what you're drawn to, what you make time for, even when it's inconvenient.

Notably, a big C Career is not a destination to be reached. It's a dynamic, evolving, fluid construct that shifts as you do. People often move between little c and big C orientations multiple times across their lives, depending on context, capacity, season, and needs.

As one participant told me, "I don't think it's either/or. I think it's about where I'm placing the center of gravity in my career right now." That's exactly the right way to think about it.

Why This Distinction Changes Everything

Once people have language for their little c and big C Careers, something shifts. They can finally name their career dilemma. What once felt confusing or shameful becomes rational. Restlessness becomes information. Ambivalence becomes a signal.

Tracy Borreson captured this moment of recognition when she said she realized she wasn't failing in her career, she was simply between orientations: not fully invested in her little c career anymore, but not yet clear on her big C Career either. Having language for that space gave her a chance to reevaluate what she was really going through.

The distinction between little c and big C Careers helps people stop misdiagnosing themselves. It reframes career confusion as a normal developmental process instead of a personal shortcoming or flaw.

Defining the Difference

Recently, my husband admitted he regretted telling me something. A friend had sent me a new job posting for a senior level leadership position at a national nonprofit with a big title and a big salary. "I shouldn't have told you to apply for that job. I realize it's going to take all your time and take you away from your big C Career. I just didn't have that language until now." Because he framed it in that way, I knew exactly what he meant. And, I knew he was right. I didn't waste my time applying.

Nora Welch was in her late thirties and in the midst of transitioning to self-employment after a decade of working in nonprofits. Self-examination had become her favorite tool for propelling her career. She told me:

> "I'm not sure I have found my big C Career yet, but I have become more aware of whether I am embodied in my work or not. I have better awareness of being either dissonant with my career or resonant with my career."

This was a major aha for Nora, trusting herself to notice if she felt resonance with her career or not as she explored what her big C Career is.

To begin defining who you are in relation to your career belonging, try this exercise. Create a chart that lists qualities of your little c career in one column and your big C Career in the other to compare them side by side.

Here's an example of what a chart might look like. It's meant to show what might come up:

Little c career	Big C Career
• Having an executive level title	• Comfortable being known for my professional identity, not my title
• Making lots of $$$	• Defining my own level of productivity and how I spend my work time each day
• GREAT benefits and unlimited paid time off	• Deciding who I work with on what terms
• Using this as a stepping stone to get a leadership role in a big tech company	• Not compartmentalizing my professional identities
• Being known as the top expert in my region	• Building relationships out of interest instead of business value
• Getting bonuses for reaching milestones	• Following my own research/ areas of interests to see where they take me
• Receiving top performance reviews of exceeds expectations	• Testing ideas without fear of failure or meeting predetermined metrics
• Working on a team of strong contributors	

Your little c career column should list what you've been told a career is, commonly external measures of success. Your big C Career column should list what a career means to you, your definitions of success based on how you see yourself in your work.

After creating both lists, ask yourself: What would it look like to shape your career with qualities more from one column than the other? The more you can define the qualities that make up your big C Career, the better you'll be able to envision it.

You should know that everyone struggles with the push and pull of navigating between a little c and big C career. That's life. It's not as simple as making two columns and then focusing on only your big C. Your big C might even sound too good to be true, too aspirational. People have told me that. Even Elise Loehnen, host of the podcast *Pulling the Thread*, who many might say is in her big C Career, once said:

> "I feel closer to my daimon [my guiding
> spirit] than I ever have, and yet I still feel
> this pull—at least twice a month—to 'give
> up on myself' and get a full-time job. It's
> easy to convince myself that it would be
> much simpler. And it would! But even that
> language—'give up on myself'—says it all."

It's possible to define your big C Career and still take jobs and make money in ways that are part of a little c career. The point is at least you'll be able to now know that's what you're doing.

By the way, careers comprise many dimensions, and if you'd like help assessing your career against these, I have a tool called the Dimensions of a Great Career. You can find it in the appendix.

At this point, you've clarified your professional identity. You've named your orientation and how you approach your career. And, you just learned two fundamentally different ways of understanding what a career can actually be.

Next, it's time to make sense of how all these pieces go together.

In the following chapter, you'll work through the Career Belonging Matrix—a tool designed to bring together your identity, your career approach, and how you want to be seen, known, and valued. This is what will help you translate your insights into direction.

Next Steps

- **Reflect**: Are you orienting primarily towards your little c career or big C Career? What signals are telling you that?

- **Define**: Name three qualities that feel essential to your big C Career. These should come from lived moments—times you felt most alive, most yourself, or most seen, known, and valued in your work.

- **Do**: Create a two column chart with the following:
    - Column A: List the forces currently shaping your little c career (titles, expectations, constraints).
    - Column B: List the forces that are part of your big C Career (values, identity, contribution).

CHAPTER 10

Step Four: Complete the Career Belonging Matrix

"The first task is to build a strong 'container'
or identity; the second is to find the contents
that the container was meant to hold."

—Richard Rohr

"There's something beautiful about choosing
yourself after spending so long doing the opposite."

—Alex Elle

If the essence of career belonging is being clear on **how you want to be seen, known, and valued in your career**—by **yourself**, by **others**, and by **something greater than you**—then the moment you can name that, you stop outsourcing your career desires to other people's expectations.

It's high time to reveal this to yourself.

A client of mine, Ala Ho, once told me she had no idea what she wanted to be seen, known, and valued for. She'd never examined herself this way.

Ala is wildly talented in music, branding, digital marketing, systems thinking, and business intelligence. She started in pre-med, switched to hospitality management, and later built a successful design agency. From the outside, she looked focused. Internally, she felt scattered and unsure of herself. She did not know what she could truly claim about herself.

Ala expressed her self-doubts to me:

> Someone asked me the other day, "What do you want to be known for?" And I couldn't answer. I'm obsessed with so many things, yet I don't feel like I can really own any of them. I don't have that ONE topic. Niching feels scary and suffocating. What do I want to be known for? What value do I want to offer? What truly brings me joy? I feel like finding clarity on these questions— discovering that thing that's unmistakably 'me'—would really help.

Ala lacked a way to translate her complexity into clarity, and that's what the Career Belonging Matrix will do for you. It makes your intangible desires, that, *"I want to feel like myself in my work,"* feeling specific enough to name, reflect on, and share with others.

If you remember, at the end of the last chapter, I asked: **How do you want to be seen, known, and valued in your big C Career?**

This chapter is where you answer that question through part one of a two-part process:

1. Complete the Career Belonging Matrix (The raw material we'll collect in this chapter)
2. Shape a master set of Seen, Known, Valued Statements (Your touchstones that we'll establish in the next chapter)

The Matrix helps you surface your truth. Your Seen, Known, Valued Statements (or I call them SKVs for short) help you remember it, repeat it, and use it. For now, let's start with the foundation.

Get Calibrated

To get the most out of the matrix, you'll need a strong sense of your professional identity and your big C Career. Otherwise, you'll accidentally fill the Matrix with generic ideas and career fit answers that don't lead to belonging.

For example, if you complete the Matrix with:

> "I see myself as a Product Director. I'm
> known as the boss. I'm valued when I hit
> quarterly goals."

Eek. That's not how you truly want to be seen, known, and valued. That's little c career compliance.

Career belonging answers sound different. They sound like your authentic professional identity in action, your ideal work experiences coming alive, and deep self awareness, like this:

- "I see myself as an inquisitive catalyst."
- "I'm known as a calm voice of reason who speaks up during hard conversations."
- "I feel valued by my coworkers as the 'team therapist' because they come to me when they're going through a rough patch."
- "I feel valued by something greater when a customer says the product I designed brought them to tears."

These kinds of responses reflect your big C Career, your professional identity, and the actual qualities that demonstrate *this work aligns with who I am.*

How The Career Belonging Matrix Works

Below is the Career Belonging Matrix. Take a moment to get acquainted with it before you answer the questions in each cell. I'll explain how it's structured, what it's designed to reveal, and how to use it in a productive way.

The Career Belonging Matrix

	BY SELF	BY OTHERS	BY SOMETHING GREATER THAN YOURSELF
SEEN	How/When do you **see** yourself in your work? What makes you **see** yourself in your work?	How/When are you seen by others in your work? What helps others see you in your work?	How/When are you seen by something greater than yourself in your work? What helps you feel seen by something greater than yourself in your work?
KNOWN	How/When do you **know** yourself in your work? What makes you **know** yourself in your work?	How/When are you known by others in your work? What makes others know you in your work?	How/When are you known by something greater than yourself in your work? What makes you feel known by something greater than yourself in your work?
VALUED	How/When do you **value** yourself in your work? What makes you **value** yourself in your work?	How/When are you valued by others in your work? What makes others value you in your work?	How/When are you valued by something greater than yourself in your work? What makes you feel valued by something greater than yourself in your work?

The Matrix is a 3x3 grid: nine cells, nine belonging insights. The rows are Seen, Known, Valued. The columns are By Self, By Others, By Something Greater Than Yourself. Each cell contains a couple corresponding questions that act as reflective prompts.

If you complete it honestly, you'll end up with a map of what career belonging actually looks like for *you*, not for somebody like you with your same job title.

Objectives of the Matrix

No matter where you are in your career, what challenges you're facing, or the unique background you have, the Career Belonging Matrix will activate clarity in your professional life and help you understand what you need to achieve a true sense of career belonging.

The Matrix has three objectives:

1. Build deeper self-knowledge and inner awareness
2. Reveal your career belonging needs (the conditions that help you thrive)
3. Give you language for what you want and need beyond "fit" so you feel more empowered to achieve it

Ultimately, if you don't know what helps you feel seen, known, and valued in your work, how will you ever recognize it, ask for it, design for it, or receive it? That's the truth.

The best part is the Matrix isn't a one-time exercise. You can return to it again and again throughout your career. The answers evolve with you. Treat the matrix as self-exploration rather than a checklist. Each iteration will provide fresh understanding because you will be a different version of yourself at a different point in your career.

Top Tips for Using the Matrix

Tip #1: Set the stage

Before starting, write your own definition of each level of belonging: self, others, and something greater than yourself, in your own words. Not mine. Doing this gets you grounded in your own thinking and definitions of these concepts.

Then take a few minutes to settle. Try a few deep breaths. Light a candle. Sit somewhere quiet. Do whatever helps you hear your inner voice. It's important to allow your intuition to speak first, and your brain to edit later. If something comes out strange, goofy, poetic, or intense, leave it. There's always space for judgment later. For now, notice what comes up.

As you embark on the matrix, start anywhere. Skip cells. Circle back. You may find that some cells resonate more than others. Some answers might take time—days, weeks, years. That's okay. The goal is not to fill out every cell of the matrix but to engage in a meaningful exploration of yourself. This might be your first time asking yourself these questions after all.

Tip #2: *Use synonyms when you get stuck*

The words *seen, known,* and *valued* are synonymous with other terms we commonly use. If these three words feel too abstract, borrow language that's adjacent. For instance, if you're unsure how you want to be "seen," try substituting the word "acknowledged" or "noticed."

Below, I grouped familiar words together as a synonym cheat sheet. If you think of other words to add to these columns, by all means, add your own. These are not fixed groupings. If you feel the word "acknowledged" is better under the "known" category, move it. The goal is to stay true to the heart of the activity, the rest is up to you.

SEEN	KNOWN	VALUED
Recognized	Remembered	Respected
Listened to	Regarded	Appreciated
Heard	Taken Seriously	Sought After
Acknowledged	Interpreted	Rewarded (financial and
Visible	Trusted	non-financial)
Noticed	"Gotten"	Invested In
Understood at	Your presence	Cared for
first glace	Noted for	Proud
Included		Accepted

Tip #3: *Keep your ego out of the driver's seat*

The Matrix is a tool for becoming more attuned, not more "important." It's not designed to help you gain fame, receive more praise, or increase your popularity.

It's healthy to want recognition and a solid personal brand. But if your answers start sounding like a resume (top performer, highest sales, featured in prestigious places) you've drifted back to career fit. Save achievements for your bio. Put your *belonging* into the Matrix.

If you would like more examples, you can reference the appendix list: "Examples of Being Seen, Known, and Valued."

Tip #4: Treat this as a living document

Right now, you might feel most seen when people refer the *perfect* work to you. Later, you might feel seen when a stranger writes to tell you your work mattered. Belonging evolves. Your responses in the matrix will evolve too, that's why it's a living document.

Complete Your Matrix

It's time to go for it!

Using a sheet of paper, a digital document, sticky notes, a spreadsheet, whatever format you like, start answering the questions in the Matrix. Follow your gut. There's no one way to do this. Let your first pass be freeform. Bullet points are fine. You'll polish and edit your answers into statements later.

Write as many responses per cell as you want. If you're drawing a blank and don't have an answer to a cell, come back to it later. You might find blind spots, which only shows where you have room to grow.

When you're finished, use the prompts below to deepen your reflection and self-inquiry.

And remember, give yourself permission to let this process take hours or days. Real answers don't often arrive on demand. They surface when you revisit them, notice prickly sensations in your body and mind, and notice when something feels off or uncertain.

Example: My Matrix

Here's what my matrix looks like in polished form so you can see the destination. Notice that some statements are general and some are specific. That's intentional. We'll talk about specificity later.

	BY SELF	BY OTHERS	BY SOMETHING GREATER THAN YOUR SELF
SEEN	I see myself as a Creative Disruptor and professional identity researcher. I bring new twists to old ideas to positively transform the world.	I feel seen by others when they introduce me as a Creative Disruptor or Professional Identity Researcher and can clearly explain what that means and why it matters.	I feel seen by something greater when a stranger reaches out for a request that's connected to my research.
KNOWN	I know myself when I refer back to a framework or tool I created as a result of my expertise as a Creative Disruptor, and it measurably helps the situation.	I feel known by others when they reach out for advice or help on something that's based on my research or writing.	I feel known by something greater when I am (or my work) is tagged or mentioned in someone else's writing or work.

	BY SELF	BY OTHERS	BY SOMETHING GREATER THAN YOUR SELF
VALUED	I value myself when I mentally pause, congratulate myself, and enjoy a moment in my work that feels highly creative, original and impactful.	I feel valued by others when they use my tools and share how they've helped them personally or professionally—whether by changing their thinking or achieving a positive outcome.	I feel valued by something greater when someone reviews my work and shares it with their audience or community simply because they find it valuable.

Reflections After Completing the Matrix

First, how did it go?

Which cells were easy? Which were hard? Where did you get stuck? What did that bring up? What's one new thing you learned about yourself? Check-in and notice how you're feeling.

Now, scan your answers in each cell: Are any themes emerging? Do you notice repeated needs, beliefs, pain points or desires?

It can be hard to answer deeply on our own. Even when we think we've fully answered, sometimes we've only scratched the surface. Here are a a few additional provocations to explore:

- Which answer surprised you most? Why? What's underneath it?
- Did you write anything bold, intense, or oddly specific? If not, why not?

- Have you ever told anyone at work what you want to be seen, known, and valued for? Why or why not?
- Do any answers scare you? Stretch you? Make you feel exposed?
- If nothing stretched you, can you add one statement that does?

Meta-Reflections After Completing the Matrix

Meta-reflection means thinking about your own thoughts. It means asking: **Why do I want this? How do I know this is true?**

For each answer you wrote in the Matrix, ask:

- Why did I write this?
- Where did this belief come from?
- What evidence is it based on?
- Is that evidence solid, biased, outdated, or borrowed?
- What changes if I revise my answer based on better evidence?

We rarely think about how we know what we know about ourselves. We tend to accept it as truth without examining why it's our truth. This step helps you replace inherited answers with more truthful ones.

Time-Based Reflections

There's one more layer to reflect on: time.

Besides meta-reflection, try answering the Matrix through three lenses:

- **Past:** When have I felt most seen/known/valued before?
- **Present:** What's true right now?
- **Future:** How do I want to feel in the next season of my career?

Time adds dimensionality and often reveals the direction your big C Career is already trying to take.

You Finished the Matrix, Now What?

After moving through the Matrix plus the additional reflections, you should have pulled a little something more out. The Matrix doesn't just capture what you think, it helps you refine what you think you *know and truly want.*

And don't forget that the sky's the limit in what counts as being seen, known, and valued for who you are in your work. It can show up in major milestones and quiet moments. In big gestures and small ones. In intentional acts, random encounters, everyday practices, and subtle nuances that are verbal or nonverbal.

The clearer you are about how you want to be seen, known, and valued, the more your sense of career belonging will expand beyond your original estimation in positive and unimagined ways. Now that you have your raw material complete, even if it seems messy and unfinished, next comes the second part of the process: turning your Matrix into a master set of useful SKV Statements.

The insights in your Matrix are essential but not enough. Career belonging requires language you can actually live by and apply. Language you can remember in a moment. Language you can share in the world.

In Chapter 11, we'll take what you wrote in the Matrix and shape it into SKVs that are clear, personal, and useful. We'll tighten them into a master set that becomes a compass for your big C Career.

Next Steps

- **Reflect**: What did you learn about yourself while completing the Matrix? Which cell felt easiest to answer, and which one (if any) did you resist?

- **Define**: Which 3–5 responses from your Matrix feel the most *potent* right now. These should feel alive and energized when you read them back, not impressive or overly future-oriented.

- **Do**: Do one "second pass" using either meta-reflection or time. Rewrite at least three of your answers based on what you discover.

CHAPTER 11

Step Five: Become Seen, Known, and Valued

"You'll never change your life until you change something you do daily. The secret of your success is found in your daily routine."

—**John C. Maxwell**

You've made it to the final step. You've completed the Career Belonging Matrix, reflected on your responses, and likely uncovered truths that took a lot of introspection, and courage, to name. What happens next builds directly on all of the self-awareness you've been cultivating across the prior steps.

Becoming seen, known, and valued is about translating what you've learned about yourself into language and behavior you can carry into conversations, decisions, and everyday moments at work. Before launching into this last piece, come ready with fresh eyes and energy.

In this chapter, you'll do three things. First, you'll create and shape a master set of Seen, Known, and Valued (SKV) statements derived from your Career Belonging Matrix. Your responses in the Matrix are the first draft of how you want to be seen, known, and valued, but they need to be polished. Second, you'll learn strategies of what it actually means to become seen, known, and valued in everyday life and in professional interactions. Third, you'll put your SKVs into action, using them as the compass that guides how you talk about your work, make decisions, and advocate for yourself so career belonging becomes something you experience daily, not just an idea in a book.

Create Your Master SKVs

I bet you have a diverse collection of answers to your Career Belonging Matrix, ranging from interesting to inspiring to deeply personal. This list is gold and a great resource in and of itself. But actualizing them is another story, that's why you'll need to pare it down to three beautifully simple and understandable statements.

If you can, make a copy of your Matrix before you start polishing it. This way you maintain the raw data you don't want to lose.

Your first goal is to reduce your answers into a master set of statements that serve as a practical tool that's easy to remember, repeat, apply, and live by. If your statements are too cumbersome or complicated, they won't be any help to you. If you have multiple responses within a single Matrix cell, try combining them into one fuller statement.

Your final set of master SKVs should include three statements:

- one for **Seen**
- one for **Known**
- one for **Valued**

Together, they function coherently. How you arrive at these three statements is up to you. For instance, you could rank your existing statements by importance. You might notice themes emerging and combine ideas together. Or you might write entirely new statements that better capture the essence of what you're trying to say across multiple cells.

What matters is that your final three SKV statements clearly express what you need to feel seen, known, and valued in your career. Only you will know when you've arrived at that mark.

An Example: My Master Set of SKV Statements

Here's my final set. Notice that my statements weave together self, others, and something greater, and that they are specific enough to be acted on.

My Master Set of SKV Statements

SEEN	KNOWN	VALUED
I see myself as a Creative Disruptor and Professional Identity Researcher. I value myself when I channel ideas into research, products and services.	I feel known by others when they repeat my tools back to me and share my insights with their circles and tell me about its impact.	I feel valued by something greater when my work becomes part of groups I've never met and I learn about it later.

You can see from mine that my *seen* statement reinforces my sense of self—my professional identity. I have certainty about who I am in my work and how I see myself professionally. I *feel* career belonging when I know who I am in my work and why it matters.

My *known statement* is around people knowing and calling me by my professional identity and also sharing things that relate to who I am. When people send me irrelevant articles or emails, or propose collaborations that don't align with my work, it makes me feel misunderstood, like they don't "get" me. It doesn't reinforce my career belonging because it shows they don't see me the way I want to be seen.

Finally, my *valued statement* is about being part of things created by other people and touching lives I may never know. I hope my research and ideas reach far and wide. My highest value is to create work that will be valuable for generations to come.

Remember, your career belonging is created by you, reflected by others, and part of something greater than yourself.

Now it's your turn, create your master set of SKV statements.

The Test: What Makes a Strong SKV Statement

Strong SKV statements aren't just aspirational or nice to say. They can be acted on by you and understood by others. If your SKVs can't guide behavior, shape decisions, or help someone know how to support you, they need more refinement.

This is where the test comes in.

Right now, your answers might be uneven: too vague, too detailed, too abstract or too long. You'll need to keep revising them to reach language that is specific, action-able, and communicable without losing their truth.

Here's what this might look like in practice. Let's say your professional identity is a *Breakthrough Idea Activator*, and you want to be seen, known, and valued for that, alongside your formal role and job title. If your Matrix response reads:

> "I feel seen by others when they appreciate
> me for my breakthrough ideas,"

That's a start, but it's still unclear. How would someone actually *do* that? What behavior would signal
appreciation?

You could refine it in a few ways:

> **Example A:** "I feel seen by others when
> I'm assigned projects that require out-of-
> the-box solutions."

> **Example B:** "I feel seen by others when
> they ask me to facilitate vision or strat-
> egy brainstorms based on complex data
> to reach novel conclusions."

Both of these versions pass the test. They are specific.
They describe observable actions. They tell others exactly
how to reflect your value back to you.

As you refine your SKVs, put yourself in the shoes
of the people in your "others" column: your manager,
boss, colleagues, clients, or collaborators. If they read
your statements, would they understand what helps you
feel seen, known, or valued? Would they know how to
respond?

Here's the simplest test of all:

> **If you, or someone else, couldn't act on
> your SKV statement, it isn't specific
> enough yet.**

Another way to test includes trying them out with people you trust and noticing their reactions. Do they get it immediately, or do they ask questions? That input is useful.

Even if your master SKV statements aren't part of your job description or performance review yet, (this is an obvious opportunity for the future), you can still communicate them to your boss, team, or followers to help them understand you more accurately now.

In fact, if you don't convey how you want to be seen, known, and valued, then it will be much harder to achieve career belonging.

Once you know your SKVs, you'll have a solid answer to the third career power question:

> "What makes you feel seen, known, and
> valued in your career?"

Your master SKV statements convey your truth in a short, tangible way. And the more you share them, the more they reinforce who you actually are.

Becoming Seen, Known, and Valued in Real Life

In *Sex & The City*, Miranda once tells Carrie, "You can't quit your column, it's who you are." Carrie looks her straight in the eye and says, "No, it's not who I am, it's what I do."

That moment mirrors the core premise of this book. When you don't define who you are in your work, others will define it for you. And most of the time, they'll base it on your job, not your identity or unique value.

Carrie knew she was more than a columnist. And by correcting Miranda, her best friend, she modeled something essential: becoming seen, known, and valued requires educating the people closest to you. Especially them.

Earlier in this book, I asked you three career power questions.

1. Who are you in your work, besides your job title?
2. What does that mean?
3. What makes you feel seen, known, and valued in your career?

At the time, you probably couldn't answer, but now you can.

So, the question remains: *how do you live your career belonging on a daily basis, in real life?*

The answer starts with you.

Career belonging isn't a one-off declaration. It's something that has to be clarified, expressed, and reinforced over time. You clarify who you are in your work and why it matters. You express that clarity through language and action. And you reinforce your identity through consistent advocacy until it becomes how you're recognized.

Here's the mantra I return to again and again with myself and with clients:

When I share how I see myself in my work,
others see me the way I want to be seen.

Until you take ownership of how you want to be perceived, others will rely on assumptions. Your master SKVs are how you express yourself so that you minimize misinterpretation.

What This Looks Like in Practice

You might find yourself crafting or revisiting your SKVs during career transitions or major career pivots, but they're meant to help you express who you are in everyday interactions: how you introduce yourself, how you attract opportunities, how you make career decisions, and how you respond when something feels off in your work.

You might use them when:

1. Looking for a new role and wanting to present yourself beyond a job title
2. Having a conversation with a manager when you feel misunderstood
3. Resetting expectations with your team, clients or collaborators
4. Proposing a professional growth path that better reflects who you are
5. Building a business or brand rooted in your professional identity

Over time, being seen, known, and valued starts to feel less abstract and becomes more tangible through work experiences like the following:

- Being **seen** might sound like a colleague introducing you in a way that reflects your professional identity, not just your role.
- Being **known** might look like being invited into rooms because of what you stand for, not just what you can execute.
- Being **valued** might show up as trust, acknowledgment, or opportunity, especially in moments that aren't tied to output.

Imagine these examples are regular occurrences that happen repeatedly because you're clear about who you are.

Notice what's absent in them: your productivity, efficiency, and speed. If you're primarily recognized for performance metrics alone, that's your career fit on display. Career belonging is about contribution, and how your presence shapes outcomes and people (not just tasks and outputs) as well as how your identity creates value.

Let SKVs Be Your Compass

Your master SKVs are a compass. They are more than words on a page. They help you prioritize and articulate what you're truly seeking. When used in the world, your SKVs shape how you present yourself, the way you discuss your career with others, and how you attract clients and opportunities that *get* you.

One of the most common mistakes I see, especially in networking and career transitions, is narrative drift. Someone introduces themselves differently depending on the audience: entrepreneur one day, strategist the next, something else entirely after that. This fuels inconsistency. Others won't know how to see or value you for who you really are.

Your SKVs reinforce your story and maintain your narrative.

Remember my master set of SKVs from earlier? Before I articulated these, people misconstrued me constantly. I learned how many assumptions were made around my research on hybrid professional identity. I was once invited to a luncheon on "professional identity" only to realize they had mistaken my expertise with identity theft issues. During the COVID-19 pandemic, hybrid work became a hot topic and people assumed I was an expert in that, not hybrid *workers*. Each time, the lesson was the same: if you don't clearly define who you are, the market will do it for you, and usually get it wrong.

I once had a boss with a long, impressive job title. In fact, it was multiple titles strung together, but she rarely used any of them. Instead, she introduced herself as, "an electrical engineer and an educator," because that's how she saw herself. She often referred to those identities when telling stories during leadership conversations,

"When I was an educator, we called those people special snowflakes because they each want personal treatment." And we respected her because of how she leveraged her professional identity instead of her job title. Years later, I still remember how she conducted herself because it was consistent and human. I felt like I knew who she was.

That's career belonging in action.

Strategies for Becoming Seen, Known, and Valued

To experience career belonging in your daily life, your SKVs need to move into action. Activating your SKVs is how you reshape your work environment, routines, brand, career path and relationships. You can infuse your SKVs into the fabric of your work in a variety of ways, but here are a few strategies to get started:

1. Share Your SKVs with Trusted People First

Talking about how you want to be seen, known, and valued can feel vulnerable at first. Start by sharing your SKVs with a trusted colleague, mentor, or friend, someone who understands your work and supports your growth. By confiding in someone you trust, you gain input and support while also reinforcing your confidence in your SKVs.

2. Make Your SKVs Visible

Create visual cues of your SKVs by writing them down and displaying them in a picture frame, on a sticky note, or on digital wallpaper. These can be private reminders for you, and public displays where others can see them.

Beyond words, consider how your physical workspace reflects your SKVs: incorporate artwork and objects, create intentional spaces, and choose furnishings as silent but powerful reinforcements of who you are and how you want to be seen.

3. Make Your SKVs Explicit

People don't often know how to provide the right support. Bring your SKVs into reviews, one-on-ones, and key conversations. This doesn't mean giving a formal presentation, although you can if you want to. It can often be as simple as weaving your SKVs into conversations with your team, manager, or clients.

4. Add Your SKVs to Your Bio

Weave your SKVs into your bio, LinkedIn profile, elevator pitch, and how others describe you when you're not in the room. Let them be present and do work for you. The more you incorporate them into your professional life, the more they become hallmarks of your reputation.

5. Build Relationships That Reinforce Them

Career belonging grows faster in environments and communities where your professional identity is recognized. Seek mentors who resonate with your SKVs. Build alliances with colleagues who accept you the way you want to be seen. Find professional networks that reflect your career interests.These could be people already on your team and also people outside your company or in other business circles.

6. Protect What Matters

If specific tasks, projects, or workplace dynamics undermine your SKVs, it's time to reconfigure them. Boundaries preserve the integrity of your career belonging. For example, if your SKVs highlight creativity but you're stuck with administrative tasks, advocate for taking on more creative projects.

7. Practice Self-Advocacy

Self-advocacy is about consistently presenting yourself in a way that aligns with your SKVs. No one will advocate for your career belonging more effectively than you. This means if you want to be seen as a thought leader, raise your hand for speaking engagements. If you want to be valued for out-of-the-box thinking, step up and facilitate more design thinking sessions.

Your Career Belonging Will Evolve

Your SKV statements will grow with you. I recommend revisiting them once a year, especially after major transitions, such as a job change or promotion. You can also reflect monthly or quarterly on what's working and where adjustments are needed. Ask yourself:

- Where do my SKVs feel most aligned?
- Where am I compromising my identity?
- What's working and what needs adjusting?

There's a lot of trial and error in this process, and some of it will likely feel strange or unfamiliar at first. Let's be honest, how often do coworkers come up to each other and say,

"I'd like to share what makes me feel seen, known, and valued in my work so you understand how I see myself and want to be recognized."

It sounds a little bananas, right?

If we stop and think about it, isn't this precisely what we're longing for? A workforce and workplaces where we don't have to guess how others want to be accepted, acknowledged and valued? A world where we can show up without assumptions, pressure to conform, or the need to mold ourselves to fit a role?

Career belonging comes from changing how you understand who you are beyond your job title. The more you journey toward that answer, the more you'll see how your career belongs to you, is reflected by others and is part of something greater than yourself.

This completes the five-step process. You've done the hard work. You've named your identity. You've articulated how you want to be seen, known, and valued. But clarity doesn't change the world around you.

Part 3 is about crossing the chasm between how you see yourself and how the world actually recognizes you. It's a literal stateshift between internal and external forces. Self-definition plays a big role, but career belonging happens when you learn how to navigate, challenge, and reshape the systems you encounter along the way. That work is ongoing, and it's where your career begins to fully belong to you.

Next Steps

- **Reflect**: Which of your master SKV statements feels easiest to put into the world first?

- **Define**: Choose one SKV strategy from this chapter and define how you might try it.

- **Do**: Take one action to advocate for your SKV statements in your current work situation.

PART THREE

CROSSING THE CHASM FROM FIT TO BELONGING

CHAPTER 12

A State Shift for All

*"When we are stricken and cannot bear our
lives any longer, then a tree has something to
say to us: Be still! Be still! Look at me! Life is
not easy, life is not difficult. Those are child-
ish thoughts... Home is neither here nor there.
Home is within you, or home is nowhere at all."*

—Herman Hesse

Whether you realize it or not, you're not the same person
as when you started this book. You've shifted in your
understanding of yourself, your professional identity, and
your career. Along the way, you've been answering hard
questions. In fact, each part of this book is about decon-
structing a key question:

Part 1 asked: *Why are you striving for career fit in the first place?*

Part 2 asked: *Who are you in your work and what do you need to achieve a sense of career belonging?*

And, Part 3 will ask: *Now that you know who you are, why will you still encounter friction instead of ease in your career?*

That's right, more friction. In theory, at this stage everything should be good to go. You've gained new language, you know yourself, and you know how to articulate how you want to be seen, known, and valued in your work. Heck, you even realize there's a difference between career fit and career belonging. This should be the moment everything snaps together and your career belonging takes shape.

Except, for most people, it's not. This is actually the moment where things get harder instead of easier, and here's why.

Even though you have more clarity and are more certain about who you are, that means you're also more aware of how it is not reflected back at you, yet. You might even feel slightly annoyed or irritated by colleagues and workplaces that once felt safe and innocuous.

This is because you're experiencing a shift in consciousness.

Educational theorist Paulo Freire describes this moment as the development of what he calls, "critical consciousness." It's when individuals develop a deepened awareness of their situation, and they begin to see their reality not as fixed or inevitable, but as historical and therefore capable of transformation. That awakening is rarely comfortable and can be destabilizing. Once you recognize the forces shaping your life and career, you cannot return to unconscious participation.

Because you see more, what you see changes you.

The career chasm lives in this space. It's a metaphorical gap between your little c career and your Big C Career, between career fit and career belonging. It's a psychological and emotional state that emerges when who you are and how you see yourself has shifted, but your life hasn't restructured around that truth yet.

The old you, before you had language for your professional identity, moved through work according to existing circumstances: job descriptions, titles, hierarchies, performance reviews, cultural expectations, and career paths. You may have felt boredom, restlessness, or dissatisfaction in your career, but you didn't have a frame of reference for what was misaligned and why things felt "off."

But now you have the tools and frameworks you were missing. That alters everything. That's why you're in a state shift. Old strategies that kept you safe like overperforming, people pleasing, and attaching worth to titles stop working, which is why it can be an intense and confusing time.

Crossing the chasm from career fit to career belonging is both an internal developmental passage as well as a negotiation between your identity shift and the systems you're part of. There is a delay in how systems understand you. This is the tension at the heart of the chasm.

You see, your critical consciousness reorganizes your internal world before your external world reorganizes around you. This gap emerges after clarity, after you know who you are, because your environment is still responding to who you *were*.

The chasm is an amplifier of how you respond to external circumstances, and it spotlights the limiting beliefs and cultural narratives you still need to address.

For jacks-of-all-trades, multipotentialites, and hybrid professionals, you'll get to know this space well. You will likely pass through the career chasm more than once. Each time, the terrain will look a little different. And each time, the stakes will feel higher because you'll have more complexity and multidimensionality to process.

How the Career Chasm Appeared in My Research

When I first began interviewing people about their careers, I didn't have a name for the career chasm. What I heard instead were stories, subtle or charged, about what I called at the time *work wounds*. This represented any unfinished business and baggage people were carrying with them: the bad boss who undermined their confidence, the colleague who got all the credit and the promotion, the insider politics and nepotism, the layoff that destroyed their sense of worth, the role that looked impressive but made them feel dead inside.

People described these experiences long after they happened because they left a deep and lasting impression on them. Work wounds shaped how they showed up, made career decisions, and what they talked about while networking. Some people were cautious and guarded. Others overcorrected by trying harder to prove themselves. And others retreated by lowering their expectations of what work they could do.

Of the people who overcame their work wounds, the common theme was moments where they said: *"This isn't who I am,"* or *"This isn't what I really want,"* or *"I can't keep pursuing this version of career success."* When old stories and professional identities loosened, their entire sense of self shifted and they were able to cross the chasm.

I realized that overcoming work wounds was a symptom of something bigger, a process people must undergo before they can entertain and fully embrace their big C Career. That's when I started referring to this as a career chasm because there is a void between what you once thought your career was and what it's becoming. Knowing this space exists gives you the knowledge and power you need to find a way through it. Otherwise, it is merely an invisible force you spend a lot of time and energy trying to figure out on your own.

Barriers That Exist in the Chasm

The career chasm causes you to address, overcome, and navigate internal barriers as well as external barriers that pull you back toward familiarity. This naturally happens when your identity clarity outpaces what workplace systems and structures understand. Crossing the chasm is about managing how safe, possible, or responsible making a career change feels at any given moment. Only you will know what moves to make and when to make them.

We all have barriers that keep us from crossing our chasm. You need to figure out which ones are blocking you so you can decide how to overcome them. Treat this process like reorganizing your closet. You have to pull everything out and see what's in there before knowing what to keep, donate, or toss. This is what it's like to overcome your career barriers.

Angel Collinson, one of the most accomplished big-mountain skiers in the world, encountered her own career chasm at the height of her success. Her story is a powerful example of how professional identity barriers can surface even when everything looks "right" from the outside. After becoming the first woman to win Powder Magazine's "Best Line" award and starring in a major ski film finale, Angel shocked the sports world by retiring at just 29. In 2021, she moved onto a sailboat with her partner and began to ask herself: *Who am I if I'm not a skier?* The first step in defining her true professional identity.

One day on her Instagram account, she spoke about how deeply she cared about what others thought. "First it was my dad, then it was pleasing sponsors, and now it's 80,000 Instagram followers...I just want to be me—all the way." This post shows Angel facing a type of barrier known as an *identity barrier.* She admitted to herself and to her followers that she has always been who others wanted her to be instead of being herself. By acknowledging this, she showed she was ready to claim her identity on her terms.

When people face unknown barriers, they tend to blame themselves for hesitating, settling, or retreating. But when people can name the barriers they're facing, they gain perspective, and with perspective, comes agency and choice.

Here is a list of the most common types of barriers:

Psychological Barriers

Fear of failure, imposter syndrome, and deeply ingrained beliefs about worth can make it difficult to trust yourself in the chasm. When you've been rewarded for fitting in or performing well within known systems, choosing something undefined can feel irresponsible or unrealistic, even when it's aligned.

Emotional Barriers

Guilt, shame, and fear of disappointing others often surface here. You may feel conflicted about leaving roles that provide stability, status, or validation, even when they no longer reflect who you are. Emotional attachments to how your career *looks* can be just as powerful as financial ones.

Practical Barriers

Money, timing, credentials, caregiving responsibilities, and logistical constraints are real. The career chasm often coincides with financial pressure, which can make exploration feel risky or indulgent. Practical barriers don't invalidate your desire for belonging, they shape the pace and pathway toward it.

Identity Barriers

One of the most difficult barriers is letting go of who you've been known as. In a little c career, identity is often tied to job titles, industries, or achievements. Releasing those labels can feel like losing a part of yourself, even when they no longer fit.

Cultural and Societal Barriers

We live in a culture that prioritizes linear progress, stability, and external success built on outdated narratives. Deviating from that script can trigger shame, judgment, or self-doubt. The pressure from dominant narratives often outweighs the permission to be honest about what's no longer working.

Workforce and Career System Barriers

We operate within workforce systems that are designed to sort, categorize, and standardize people, not to understand them. Hiring processes, job descriptions, resumes, promotion structures, and AI reward predefined roles. When your professional identity is multidimensional, these systems struggle to understand your value.

Every one of these barriers pulls you back toward career fit, even when you've outgrown it or sworn it off. If that happens to you, it doesn't mean you're incapable or lacking courage, it means you're navigating powerful forces and trying to honor who you are becoming. Crossing the chasm is big work that requires big commitment and does not happen overnight. Your awareness of the career chasm and the barriers within it are the foundation for moving towards your big C Career.

Crossing the Career Chasm Is a Process of Becoming

Identity researchers have long described periods of stagnation, suspension, and experimentation within our lives and careers. James Marcia refers to them as "moratoriums"—seasons of exploration before new identity commitments solidify. Herminia Ibarra writes about "provisional selves," the identities we try on as we evolve. Both emphasize that identity development is a progression that happens over our lifetime.

Achieving career belonging is an evolving relationship between yourself and the work systems you navigate to be seen, known, and valued on your terms. Knowing that the career chasm exists and that it's a state shift for all is a critical element to comprehend. This is the final piece in removing the friction that stands in your way.

In the coming chapters, I'll discuss the state shift in more detail across three key areas: what the career chasm requires of you personally, how it affects your relationships with others, and what it signals about the future of work itself. This will help you perceive the larger interrelatedness and connections that must happen across all levels of belonging in order to transform careers as we know them.

Next Steps

- **Reflect**: How are you experiencing the gap between who you now know yourself to be and how your work or environment still reflects who you used to be?

- **Define**: Name the primary barriers you are facing in the career chasm: psychological, emotional, practical, identity-based, or cultural, and how each one is influencing your decisions.

- **Do**: Choose one barrier to work with this week and take a small step that honors your professional identity.

The Shift for Yourself

*"The difference between the right word
and the almost right word is the difference
between lightning and a lightning bug."*

—Mark Twain

What does crossing the chasm require of you? When you're in the career chasm, it can feel like ambling through a dense fog or stumbling through a dark wood without any clue of where you're going. It's normal to wonder whether you were more secure before you began this journey and developed a new level of critical consciousness and self-awareness. It doesn't feel like growth or transformation at the outset. But being in the chasm is part of reorganizing your self-concept and becoming more connected to your sense of self, and that's why it is ultimately a growth process.

The chasm will test you. There will be moments of second-guessing, self-doubt, and identity fatigue as you hold onto your authentic professional identity before it has been fully validated externally in your work.

On an intuitive level you know who you are, but your brain craves testimonials and hard evidence for reassurance. You may be tempted to revert back to old roles and titles simply because they are familiar to you and others. It's not a failure if you give into this urge as long as you're mindful of why you're doing it, that's what makes this a process.

This chapter focuses on how to manage this state shift for yourself and provides a number of research-backed tools to try during this process.

Main Takeaways: Focus on Healing and Reducing Stress

You have two main jobs to do in the career chasm: 1) heal and 2) manage your stress response. Cultural critic bell hooks writes that healing begins when we honor every part of who we are. That principle applies to professional identity development as well. Hooks says:

> *"Often we hear that we must give up parts*
> *of ourselves to achieve peace or stabil-*
> *ity in life. But true healing, true recovery,*

*comes when we honor every part of who
we are—the messy, the difficult, the joyful,
and the tender. This act of self-recovery is
what allows us to live fully, rather than
just survive."*

Listen to this advice. To successfully cross the chasm, it's not about willpower, working harder, bold decisions, aha moments, starting from scratch, or the perfect plan. It's a healing process. Crossing the chasm happens by adopting tiny habits and practices that help you stay more connected to yourself, while moving through a rigid workforce filled with narrow narratives.

Physiologically, the career chasm destabilizes old beliefs and patterns that your nervous system relied on. That disruption activates your stress response. Stress pushes you into familiar coping states, and you default to what once helped you survive or stay employed.

You may remember the nine states of career being from Chapter 7. Those states appear in the career chasm. You may find yourself in career fight, feeling compelled to push harder or prove yourself. You might be in career flight, trying to leave roles abruptly, chase new opportunities, or run toward the next thing in the hope that motion will restore clarity. Or you might find yourself in career freeze, knowing something needs to change, but you can't move yet.

How your nervous system responds to the chasm is unique to you, but it's likely you'll experience some form of stress. The goal is to recognize if you're stressed and what kind of stress response you're experiencing. Then you can decide how to proceed.

Crossing My Own Career Chasm

When I entered my greatest career chasm (yes, I've been through more than one), I was in my early forties. I had been laid off and was struggling to land offers. I said yes to anything that promised relief in the form of income or assurance I was still employable. I applied for roles that made sense on paper but not in my heart. I explored paths that sounded strategic but felt empty. From the outside, I looked busy and proactive. Inside, I felt disconnected from myself. I was stressed beyond comfort and squarely in career fright.

When I still wasn't getting offers, I slid into career freeze, and then panic sent me into career flight. I felt increasingly desperate and impatient. I second-guessed my instincts. I worried I was unemployable. I became careful with what I said, and preoccupied with how I might be perceived if I did the wrong thing. I stopped listening to my intuition. I treated it as unreliable and impractical.

The turning point came when I was on the verge of a big decision. I was preparing to sell my home and belongings and start over someplace new where nobody knew me. It would have given me temporary security, but required a huge sacrifice. I had hit my rock bottom, but something inside me kept saying, *"Wait a little longer. Don't sell it yet."*

I decided to wait a month, and that pause changed everything because it signaled to my nervous system that I was ready to let go without doing something I might regret. I wasn't trying to hold onto anything any longer: stuff, identities, or expectations. That's when I started noticing subtle shifts.

I grew more confident saying no without wondering if I was turning something down. With no F's left to give, I felt more freedom. I stopped applying to every job because I knew it was actually making me feel worse instead of creating momentum. That pause gave me space to start healing. Over time, a couple opportunities showed up. In fact, a bridge role surfaced with a startup that paid enough to stabilize my finances and ease my insecurity. Once I started that role, on the side, I was able to put energy into More Than My Title, not as an entrepreneurial leap, but as a natural expression of who I am and the work that reflected my true professional identity.

I only stayed with the startup for a few months before another door opened. For the first time, my career felt like an extension of who I am rather than something I was doing for others.

Crossing that career chasm taught me how to stay connected to myself, my inner voice, and innate wisdom, while navigating unpredictable work opportunities. This is what allowed me to move closer to career belonging. I could tell something else was possible besides career fit.

For me, even as the author of this research, career belonging is something I continue to work on daily as a practice. I am still healing my past work wounds even as I feel the pull of career fit, but I'm better at noticing old tendencies and making smarter decisions that keep me aligned with who I really am.

Lived Examples of Crossing the Career Chasm

Nicholas Whitaker: Belonging on His Terms

You may remember Nicholas from Chapter 1. When he was laid off from Google, the loss disrupted more than his job. It destabilized the identity he had built around competence, status, and external validation.

In the months that followed, Nicholas entered the career chasm. Rather than rushing to replicate his previous role, he spent time reflecting on who he was outside of the systems that had defined him.

Today, Nicholas coaches midlife professionals and is a co-founder of a nonprofit focused on rethinking work. His career now integrates leadership, mindfulness, and community-building as an extension of who he has been all along. His work is in alignment with his professional identity because he feels seen, known, and valued.

Yael Gavish: Choosing Patience Over Optics

For Yael, whom I also mentioned in Chapter 1, the career chasm lasted years, not months. On paper, her career looked ideal: senior executive roles, strong compensation, great teams. But internally, she felt blah.

Yael describes it this way:

> On paper, it was great—a senior executive role at a tech startup, a fortune in stock options, a great team... but I knew something was missing. This was my third job in as many years, so it wasn't them, it was me—I couldn't bear to spend 9+ hours a day every day on something that felt so...flat.

Rather than rushing into the next obvious step, Yael chose patience. She spent years studying, experimenting, and listening to what consistently pulled at her sense of aliveness. Eventually, she returned to what she had long denied:

> I realized what I truly wanted to do in my life—what I had always wanted to do but kept denying: art and design. This journey also led me to write what I was learning, which led me to start a blog, which led me to realize that I want to give people what I

wish I had when I quit my job—a playbook
for how to go from a life that looks great
on paper but lacks a sense of purpose and
aliveness, to a life they're in love with.

Today, Yael creates large-scale minimalist art and writes
about the journey of choosing meaning and following
your intuition. Her story illustrates that refusing to rush
is sometimes the most courageous move toward career
belonging.

Elise Loehnen: Re-authoring the Story

When Elise entered her forties, she believed her most
productive years were behind her. Despite an impressive
career as an editor, content executive, and ghostwriter,
she felt disconnected from her own authorship.

She describes that feeling with honesty:

> I'd ghostwritten twelve books and had
> only ever worked for other people and
> brands. I was angry with myself that I'd
> 'wasted' the most productive period of my
> life with nothing to show for it.

Rather than chasing new titles or external validation,
Elise began choosing projects that genuinely energized
her. Over time, she realized the story she was telling
herself no longer matched reality.

I've built an encyclopedia of content that I actually own. And I did all of this while lamenting the loss of the most productive years of my life. It makes no sense because it was a really stupid story.

Today, Elise is a writer, editor, and host of the podcast *Pulling the Thread*, and a New York Times bestselling author. By re-authoring her career narrative, she moved from career fit to career belonging.

Shelley Paxton: Leaving the Script Behind

Shelley followed what she calls her "dad's success script" all the way to becoming CMO of Harley-Davidson. Shelley explained:

> It served me very, very well until it didn't. I got to this incredible place…and according to all the boxes on the success script, I should be walking on water. But I wasn't. I felt empty inside and couldn't put words to that. That's what led me to this idea that we can do all the things, but if we're doing them based on everything outside of us, which is the traditional success script, it can leave us feeling success 'empty.'

Her career chasm began when she realized this:

If we truly want to be successful, then it
has to come from the inside out. That's
what career belonging is to me.

Today, Shelley is an author, advisor, and keynote speaker whose work helps others question inherited success scripts and redefine success on their own terms. Her motto is "I quit so you don't have to." Her book, *Soulbbatical: A Corporate Rebel's Guide To Finding Your Best Life,* inspires rebels to unite and pursue a life that is truly success-FULL.

These stories offer a glimpse of what crossing the chasm to career belonging looks like in real life. They represent people who stayed true to themselves long enough for their career belonging to take shape. They didn't undergo dramatic reinventions overnight to get there.

Tools for Crossing the Career Chasm

Traditional career tools are designed to achieve outcomes based on the goal of career fit. They optimize your resume, accelerate your search, assign you a profile based on a psychographic assessment, or push you toward premature certainty in your decisions. However, starting the process instead with professional identity clarity means you learn to understand your identity shift first so you can reorganize your career around it. That's why traditional career tools are better used afterwards, otherwise they create more pressure.

Below is a set of tools to support specific professional identity challenges that arise in the career chasm. They will help you heal old work wounds and regulate your stress response so you don't fall back towards career fit. These tools address things like urgency, self-doubt, over-efforting, paralysis, or the temptation to abandon yourself for security, the inner realities of career transformation.

As you cross the chasm, the goal is to find what helps you stay aligned to who you are/are becoming so that your big C Career can take shape. You don't need to use every single tool listed below; some will resonate immediately, others may become useful later.

Also, remember to reference the barriers listed in Chapter 12: psychological, emotional, practical, identity, and societal/cultural. That list reminds you which barriers you're up against so you can choose the right tool for you.

Tool 1: Choose Stillness and Solitude Before Momentum

After gaining professional identity clarity, many people feel pressure to move straight into action. They want to fix, update, and start promoting their new identity everywhere. But rushing often reinforces career flight rather than integration.

Alex Elle, author of *How We Heal*, describes reaching a moment in her mid-thirties when she realized she had settled into environments and patterns that no longer supported her. Rather than rushing toward the next identity or opportunity, she made a conscious decision to enter what she called a "season of stillness."

> "Finding our way is hard when we're emotionally stuck in certain habits, relationships, and environments. Choosing to unstick myself required that I look at my life and connections holistically to understand where I truly wanted to go."

Alex made a conscious intention to re-prioritize herself and not stay anywhere longer than she should. During this time, she spent more time alone to gain clarity, taking walks and meditating to lose the extra weight she had gained in her mind, body, and spirit. Through daily practices to get unstuck, she built greater emotional resilience, mental clarity, and alignment with her true self. It was a turning point for Alex and not a temporary commitment.

This supports Carl Jung's belief that solitude is essential for individuation. Jung wrote that only by being alone with oneself can we discover what supports us when familiar structures fall away. In the career chasm, solitude creates the conditions for identity integration rather than reactive decision-making. Solitude supports nervous system regulation, identity consolidation, and discernment. It is a stabilizing force, not a retreat.

Stillness and solitude don't mean stopping forever, opting out, or being by yourself. It's about making space to create internal quiet so you can hear what your inner voice is asking before taking your next step.

Tool 2: Grieve the Identities You Are Outgrowing

One of the most common challenges of the career chasm is grief. In *Working Identity*, organizational psychologist Herminia Ibarra explains that career transitions require letting go of old identities before new ones fully form. This in-between period can feel disorienting because you are no longer who you were, but you are not yet fully who you are becoming.

Anthropologist Mary Catherine Bateson describes this grieving process as active meaning-making. We are constantly composing our lives, arranging experiences into narratives that help us understand who we are. When an identity no longer fits, grief is not a sign of failure. It is part of narrative reorganization.

Taking time to grieve outdated identities allows you to stop performing versions of yourself that no longer belong to you. Without this process, many people remain tethered to who they were simply because it feels familiar. You have to let go of versions of yourself that were rewarded and admired while learning how to accept the version of yourself that the world hasn't validated yet. Believing in your true professional identity takes time and courage.

Tool 3: Re-author Your Career Story

How you tell your career story shapes how you move forward. Psychologist Dan McAdams' research on narrative identity shows that people who experience their lives as meaningful tend to tell *redemptive* stories—narratives in which difficult experiences lead to growth, agency, and contribution.

In contrast, "contamination" stories frame setbacks as proof that something is wrong with you or that your best years are behind you. Crossing the career chasm requires revisiting the stories you tell about your work:

- What did that layoff *mean*?
- What did that role *teach* you?
- What patterns are emerging when you look across your career as a whole?

Re-authoring your story does not mean rewriting history. It means reclaiming yourself.

Tool 4: Identify and Meet Unmet Career Needs

Marshall Rosenberg, the founder of Nonviolent Communication, says, "Every criticism, judgment, diagnosis, and expression of anger is the tragic expression of an unmet need." In the career chasm, frustration, resentment, or exhaustion are often signals that core career needs—autonomy, recognition, creativity, safety, impact—are not being met.

Instead of treating these emotions as problems to eliminate, invite yourself to listen to them as information. Naming unmet needs helps you move from self-blame to self-responsibility and from reaction to choice. These unmet needs may also influence how you write SKV statements.

Tool 5: Reduce Blind Spots Through Greater Self-Awareness

Psychologist Tasha Eurich's research shows that while most people believe they are self-aware, only a small percentage actually are. In the career chasm, blind spots can pull you back into familiar roles or patterns without you realizing it.

A tip Eurich recommends is shifting from "why" questions–which often lead to rumination–to "what" questions that promote clarity and action. For instance, "What can I do?" versus "Why am I unhappy?" Also, be careful of being too introspective without seeking regular external feedback.

This tool encourages calibrated self-awareness: reflection paired with feedback and insight paired with reality-testing. Self-awareness is not about over-analyzing yourself. It's about seeing yourself clearly to make informed decisions.

Tool 6: Combine Self-Control with Self-Efficacy to Stay Motivated

Self-control involves regulating your emotions, resisting distractions, and persevering through adversity. Self-efficacy is your belief in your ability to succeed in specific tasks or situations. Psychologist Albert Bandura's research on self-efficacy shows that individuals who believe they can influence outcomes are more likely to persist through uncertainty and seek growth opportunities.

Combining self-control and self-efficacy—strengthening impulse control, practicing delayed gratification, and enhancing emotional regulation—can make you more resilient as you cross your chasm.

Tool 7: Use Imagination to Expand Possibility

Psychotherapist Esther Perel reminds us that imagination is essential when certainty is unavailable. Without it, fear narrows our options and keeps us bound to what is already known.

Imagination allows you to envision forms of work that do not yet exist, roles that are not yet named, and careers that are designed rather than inherited. In the career chasm, imagination creates room for belonging to emerge.

These tools are meant to help you stay connected to yourself while your career reorganizes around who you are becoming. When people use them, something subtle but important happens. They stop reacting to the chasm as a problem to escape and start relating to it as a space they can move through with intention.

Closing Thoughts

The work is about noticing your discomfort as evidence that your inner life has outpaced your external environment. When you learn how to stay connected to yourself inside the chasm, you stop mistaking stress for stagnation, misalignment, and misdirection. You start seeing it as a signal that healing and growth are underway. Noticing discomfort instead of getting swallowed up by it will help you move forward. See this as a developmental passage.

Aside from what you need to focus on for yourself, the next question becomes: ***What happens when you stay steady in your identity long enough for the external world to respond?*** That's where we're headed next. It's time to look outward. Chapter 14 will discuss the external arc where the workforce structures begin to bend.

Next Steps

- **Reflect**: Where are you experiencing stress, urgency, or self-doubt in the career chasm, and how is your nervous system responding (fight, flight, or freeze)?

- **Define**: Identify one pattern, story, or outdated identity you are currently holding onto that no longer reflects who you are becoming.

- **Do**: Choose one practice from this chapter (stillness, grieving, re-authoring, naming unmet needs, or self-awareness) and integrate it into your week as a way to stay connected to yourself, not to force progress.

CHAPTER 14

The Shift for Others

*"It is a peculiar sensation, this double
consciousness, this sense of always looking
at one's self through the eyes of others, of
measuring one's soul by the tape of the world
that looks on in amused contempt and pity."*
—W.E.B. Du Bois

Once your professional identity is clear, it changes how you see yourself and how you describe yourself to others.

When I meet someone new, I tell them, "I'm Sarabeth, and I call myself a Creative Disruptor." This is who I am (and, honestly, who I've always been without knowing it). It took me twenty years of work experience to figure out this identity language and express it with certainty.

I used to feel guilty about being a disruptor. Disruption was framed as a liability, a problem, something to avoid. I was told that I was pushy. Too intense. Too much. My creative brainstorms were minimized for being too outlandish and unrealistic. And yet, those same traits were responsible for the most meaningful impact I made in past roles. I created new tools, processes, and experiences no one had tried before or even envisioned. Being a disruptor was my strength, even when others treated it as a problem.

Over time, I hid and downplayed parts of myself because the systems around me did not know how to value them. Being a "Creative Disruptor" didn't fit neatly into my job description or align with my performance metrics, and so it stayed hidden. It took me a long time to legitimize my professional identity as the reason I'm a smart hire in the first place.

When you begin using professional identity language rather than job titles, the people and workforce systems around you—also known as the hiring processes, performance frameworks, organizational charts, clients searching for services, etc.—are not ready for it. They're not designed to orient around your professional identity. They assess you based on whether you're the right fit, a strong match, and much of that assessment comes down to simplifying complexity into recognizable categories and keyword search terms.

That's why when you present yourself by showing your multidimensional, hybrid nature, the disconnect you experience is not about communication, it's about systems and perception.

The deeper question becomes:

> *What do others (and the workforce systems I'm part of) currently perceive? And what would have to shift for them to see me the way I see myself?*

This is what the state shift for others is about. To understand this better, look at Neri Oxman.

Neri is often described as an architect, a designer, or a scientist. None of those labels are wrong, but none of them are sufficient. Trained in architecture in Israel and later earning a PhD at MIT, she went on to found the Mediated Matter group at the MIT Media Lab. Her work combines computational design, material science, biology, ecology, and fabrication. She coined the term "Material Ecology" to describe what she was building—a field that refused the separation between form and function, nature and machine, design and science. Neri is the epitome of someone who defies categorization and labels.

There are documented interviews where Neri explains that her work is often miscategorized as: "Just design," "Just art," or "Just architecture" even though it integrates engineering, biology, computation, and fabrication. Her work has been exhibited at MoMA, she has been featured on the cover of *Wired*, and her pieces live in the Smithsonian. Neri is an enigma. Her professional identity does not fit neatly into any single category; some say she's a unicorn. But she's not. She's not only multitalented, she's a hybrid professional.

Even though it appears she's transcended categories, she's had to navigate a variety of workforce systems and structures in her career. Universities are organized by disciplines, yet Neri is interdisciplinary. Funding streams are categorized by field, yet Neri works across four fields simultaneously. Tenure committees evaluate within established boundaries and academic legitimacy flows through departmental silos, yet again Neri is boundaryless.

Her work required an institutional space that could allow and perceive her synthesis. The MIT Media Lab, known for its interdisciplinary structure and project-based research model, offered that space. It was not that traditional departments suddenly evolved to interpret her differently. It was that she found and built within a structure designed to recognize integration rather than specialization.

The lesson here is you either have to find a place that understands you, create one, change the system, or, make it stretch to meet you where you are.

Who Are "The Others"?

When I use the terms "others," I mean specific roles inside workforce systems that hold power over your career and how you're seen, known, and valued. The others includes:

- AI tools and agents
- Hiring managers
- Direct managers
- HR and People Operations leaders
- Promotion and tenure committees
- Executive leadership teams
- Clients and investors
- Even your own colleagues

Each of these groups participates in interpreting you, making sense of and making meaning of who you are in your work and what your value is. Each one decides, in explicit and implicit ways, which category you belong to, what value you create, and how you're seen inside their system.

Importantly, each of them operates under clear constraints:

> **AI tools and agents** are trained on existing data and patterns. They are designed based on what has been seen and labeled before, not to interpret nuance, context, or emerging identities. As

a result, they tend to reinforce existing categories rather than recognize complexity.

Hiring managers are under time pressure. They are sorting through dozens or hundreds of applicants and are incentivized to reduce risk. They are not rewarded for deciphering complexity; they are rewarded for making defensible decisions.

Direct managers are measured by team output. They need clarity of role to hit quarterly targets. When someone expands beyond a job description, it can feel destabilizing to a structure built on predictable deliverables.

HR and People Operations teams build competency frameworks, leveling systems, and compensation bands. These systems must scale across hundreds or thousands of employees. To scale, they rely on standardization. Standardization requires categories.

Promotion committees justify advancement decisions using documentation, peer comparisons, and precedent. They look for recognizable progression. They ask: Does this person look like others who have succeeded here before?

Clients and investors evaluate you through market positioning. They want to know quickly: What do you do? Where do you fit? Why should we trust you?

None of these groups are inherently resistant to you or your growth. Most of them are intelligent, thoughtful people or technologies. But they are embedded in structures that prioritize clarity and categorization over nuance and uniqueness. They are incentivized to choose recognizable trajectories over nonlinearity and nonconformity.

So when you begin articulating how your professional identity is about integrating instead of specializing, you are asking these systems, these groups, to perceive something they were not explicitly designed to detect. This is the interpretation gap—the state shift—and it causes friction.

Until you understand who holds the power to interpret and do sensemaking of your environment, and what constraints shape their perception, you will continue mistaking structures that reduce you for personal misunderstanding and devaluation. **The state shift for others begins by recognizing the friction is not only about how well you explain yourself, it is also about what the system has the capacity to perceive.**

Why Others Are Trained to Misrecognize

When a manager asks you to "focus," a recruiter tells you your background is "interesting, but unclear," a colleague introduces you using your old title instead of the language you now use, or a performance review highlights what's missing instead of what you synthesize, it feels like rejection, dismissal, minimization, or devaluation of who you are.

In many cases, what you're experiencing is not interpersonal resistance, it's structural misrecognition. Workforce systems are designed to reduce ambiguity and de-risk. When roles, reporting lines, and performance metrics are clear, organizations function more predictably.

When your professional identity defies categorization, evaluation becomes harder:

- How do we measure this person?
- How do we compensate them?
- Where do they sit in the org chart?
- What precedent do we use?

So the system nudges you back toward clarity, not your clarity, but its clarity. This is when flattening happens.

- Your complexity gets translated into one of the closest available categories.
- Your role becomes "project management."
- Your superpower in opportunity translation becomes "operations."

- Your interdisciplinary abilities become "creative" or "collaborative."

It isn't that others cannot appreciate your complexity, it's that the tools they are given to interpret you are limited. The interpretation gap doesn't happen accidentally. It's produced. Workforce systems are designed to make decisions at scale. To do that, they require simplification and classification. Think about how careers are structured inside most organizations:

- Job descriptions define static role containers.
- Competency frameworks categorize skills into predefined buckets.
- Performance reviews evaluate output against narrow functional expectations.
- Succession plans map vertical progression within departments.
- Compensation bands tie pay to titles, not contribution complexity.
- Applicant tracking systems filter resumes through keyword detection.
- Organizational charts prioritize hierarchy over fluidity.

Every one of these tools serves a purpose. They create order. They reduce ambiguity. They make large groups manageable. But they also train on what is seen, known, and valued. They teach recruiters what counts as relevant. They teach HR how to measure performance. They teach employees what kinds of growth are rewarded.

And what is rewarded? *Predictability. Specialization. Clear trajectories. Replicable skill sets.*

And, what do they struggle to perceive? *Multidimensionality. Hybridity. Cross-functional synthesis. Interdisciplinary expertise. Nonlinear arcs. Identity evolutions.*

When your professional identity defies classification, you are asking systems built for categorization to detect what makes your uniqueness valuable. And most cannot. Reduction happens because interpretation must occur quickly. A hiring manager looks at your resume for six seconds. An AI parser looks at it for milliseconds. A performance review must be justified in a rating grid. A promotion decision must withstand scrutiny and precedent. In these moments, complexity is filtered and classified. If your identity expands beyond your role, the system simply doesn't register you.

The friction feels like this: A manager may genuinely value you, yet still evaluate you using a competency matrix that cannot capture complexity. A recruiter may be intrigued by your background, but unable to route you into a pipeline because no requisition matches your integration. Hence, you are justified in feeling unseen. The system isn't designed to see or make sense of you and your value.

What Must Shift in Systems

Most workforce systems are optimized for sorting. They are built to answer:

- Is this person qualified?
- Do they fit?
- Can they perform the tasks associated with this title?

But career belonging requires different questions:

- What contribution does this person make when their full professional identity is engaged?
- What becomes possible in this system when this person's hybridity is activated?
- How does this person create value across domains, not just within a single role?
- What capacity does this person add to the system that is not visible in their job title?

For managers, this means learning to evaluate contribution beyond task execution. It requires noticing synthesis, cross-functional thinking, pattern recognition, and identity-driven initiative, not just output aligned to job descriptions within a predefined lane.

For HR and People Operations leaders, it means examining whether competency frameworks are overly narrow. Do leveling systems reward integration? Do performance reviews allow space to describe multidimensional value? Are promotion criteria tied exclusively to vertical specialization, or do they recognize lateral expansion and synthesis?

For executive teams, it means asking whether organizational charts are containers or constraints. Does the structure allow roles to evolve as people evolve? Is internal mobility possible across domains, or only upward within silos?

For recruiters and hiring managers, it may mean loosening rigid keyword dependency and experimenting with contribution-based evaluation. Instead of asking, "Has this person done this exact job before?" the question becomes, "Can this person integrate these domains in a way this organization has not yet seen?"

This is not about abandoning structure. Organizations need clarity. They need role definition. But they also need adaptability. When professional identity expands beyond structural perception, organizations risk losing precisely the kind of multitalented, integrative thinkers they claim to value.

Career belonging at scale would require systems that:

- Emphasize contribution rather than static task lists
- Reward integrative or interdisciplinary thinking in performance assessments

- Support nonlinear role evolution, not just vertical promotion
- Recognize professional identity evolution over time, not just job title promotions
- Create space for hybrid and cross-functional pathways

None of these shifts are radical. They are incremental improvements to existing structures, and they matter because workforce systems shape what kinds of professional identities feel viable.

When systems only perceive specialization, people collapse into it. When systems reward integration, complexity becomes sustainable. The state shift for others is not about teaching every organization to perfectly understand every individual. It is about increasing the system's ability to perceive what already exists.

When perception expands, belonging becomes possible.

Final Thoughts

The modern workforce was designed around specialization, industrial efficiency, and stable career ladders. But roles are blurring, titles have become meaningless, technology is accelerating interdisciplinary solutions, portfolio careers are proliferating, and artificial intelligence is automating narrow expertise while amplifying synthesis.

In this current state, knowing who you are beyond a job title (aka your professional identity) is not an indulgence, it's an adaptation to outdated systems that are miscategorizing talent into what they need.

If you have been pigeonholed, miscategorized, or had to abandon parts of yourself in a role, it shows that the systems you are operating inside of have limited you. The state shift for others begins with realizing that achieving career belonging depends on the capacity of others and workforce systems to interpret you effectively and accurately, so you're no longer misrecognized and undervalued. Start by asking, "*What can this system currently perceive?*" to understand what you're up against.

The question we must all ask is, "*Can our workforce systems evolve quickly enough to understand the complexity of modern talent, so people and systems don't suffer from mass fit and blanding at scale?*"

Chapter 15 explores what that evolution looks like. If career belonging is to become more than an individual resilience strategy, what must change at the level of institutions, leadership, and culture? What does a workforce look like when it is designed not just to sort talent into boxes, but to recognize uniqueness and how to catalyze its potential?

The future of work will be shaped by who and what we choose to see.

Next Steps

- **Reflect**: Where in your career are you being misunderstood, flattened, or miscategorized, and how can you reinterpret that as a systems issue?

- **Define**: Identify the key "others" in your situation (manager, hiring system, client, etc.) and the constraints shaping how they are able, or unable, to perceive your full professional identity.

- **Do**: Choose one system you're operating in and decide whether to adapt to it, stretch it, or seek a different one that can better recognize your professional identity. For example: your resume, performance review, or personal website

The Shift for the Future of Work

"A search for daily meaning as well as daily bread, for recognition as well as cash, for astonishment rather than torpor; in short, for a sort of life rather than a Monday through Friday sort of dying."

—*Studs Terkel*

The future of work hinges on a new question. We need to shift from asking, *"Where does this person fit?"* to *"How well can our systems understand who this person is and who they are becoming in their work?"*

The future of work will be shaped by our ability to build systems that can recognize *who* someone actually is beyond job titles, resumes, and skills. When unnamed or invisible professional identities become clearer, people can be valued more accurately instead of reduced to labels and narrow measures of fit.

This chapter looks at what must change, what needs to be on our radar now, and which design principles can guide us toward a workforce that better understands people in their work. To get there, we first need to name what our current systems still cannot see.

What Work Systems Cannot Yet See

Being misunderstood in your work is not a personal anomaly. It reflects a structural disconnect between how careers have evolved and how society still assesses people. Today's candidates often share the same degrees, similar pedigrees, nearly indistinguishable competency profiles, and identical job titles. Search any common title on LinkedIn and the repetition becomes obvious. Professionals try to stand out inside systems built to sort and filter, yet often end up looking interchangeable on paper or filtered out altogether.

At a systems level, we evaluate people against established criteria, which leaves little room for emergent or hidden qualities that are sui generis: uncategorizable, or belonging to a class of one's own. The consequences extend far beyond individual frustration. They include systemic losses: underutilized talent, stalled advancement, disengagement, burnout, drift, lower lifetime earnings, and abandoned potential.

For decades, workforce infrastructure has operated on a simple logic: match talent to roles, train for tasks, reward specialization, advance people up hierarchical tracks, and assume coherence from a resume. That logic made sense in industrial and early knowledge economies, but it makes less sense now.

What work systems still cannot see is that people who defy categorization are becoming the norm, not the exception. Modern professionals have moved beyond binary classifications like expert or generalist. Increasingly, they are both/and workers who contain multitudes in uncommon and rare combinations. Yet, we have no shared processes for how to develop, hire, manage, train, and advance "both/and" people as an acknowledged aspect of the workforce.

Those who identify as multi-hyphenates, polymaths, jacks-of-all-trades, and hybrid professionals represent a growing segment of workers. Examples of this include professionals whose roles integrate across domains such as biogeochemical engineering, computational evolutionary theory, climate finance, and digital therapeutics. Or those whose career trajectories involve moving between sectors, stacking disparate credentials, building portfolio careers, and undergoing multiple professional pivots over longer lifespans. These examples signify significant shifts in how people work, and now systems are lagging in their ability to assess and interpret them.

Today's workforce systems and tools were never designed to see or look for interconnections across someone's work experiences, talents, degrees, ways of thinking, values, and contributions in a meaningful way that processes them as a coherent whole.

What systems cannot yet see is that when matching, profiling, and sorting remain the dominant logic of workforce design, five predictable outcomes follow:

1. **We produce professional blanding at scale.** Professional identity erosion and devaluation happen as people compress themselves into keywords, repeat marketable phrases, and converge toward sameness to remain legible. Distinctiveness is suppressed or edited out altogether.

2. **We misallocate talent.** People who are interdisciplinary are evaluated as generalists. Translators are labeled as connectors. Hybrid thinkers are slotted into narrow roles that use only a fraction of their capacity.

3. **We reward conformity.** Systems favor those who align neatly with predefined pathways over those who create new ones.

4. **We miss integrative value.** The capacity to connect silos, synthesize disciplines, and operate across boundaries becomes invisible because it does not fit inside traditional competency grids.

5. **We build brittle organizations.** When everyone is optimized for a narrow slice of expertise–and advancement depends on fitting preexisting molds–adaptability weakens, innovation slows, resilience declines.

These consequences are already shaping hiring pipelines, leadership benches, and organizational cultures.

What work systems cannot yet see is that professional identity must be the new orientation point of value. To start questioning our perceptions and design new ways of seeing who workers actually are, let's discuss three key structural shifts to make this happen.

Shift #1: From Fit to Belonging

If the future of work is about creating better ways to perceive talent, then being seen, known, and valued is the outcome of getting that perception right. This requires shifting career systems away from fit, which assumes people should adapt themselves to what already exists, and moving towards belonging.

As I stated in Chapter 2, belonging is a broad concept. When most people hear the word *belonging*, they think of culture. They think of inclusion initiatives, team cohesion, psychological safety, and whether employees feel welcomed inside an organization. That is workplace belonging, which is about feeling accepted inside a specific environment shaped by team norms and leadership behavior.

However, you can be included on a team and still feel misinterpreted in your career. You can enjoy your coworkers and still feel professionally misunderstood. You can receive positive performance reviews and still feel undervalued.

That's why career belonging operates at a deeper layer. Career belonging is an enduring sense of being seen, known, and valued across the entire arc of your professional life, no matter what jobs you hold, teams you're on, or employers you work for.

It is about whether your professional identity is reflected by others and connected to something larger than yourself. This distinction matters because career belonging is not a soft addition to the future of work. It is structural and fundamental.

Fit asks, *"Do you match what we already understand?"*

Belonging asks, *"How can we understand and accept you as you are?"*

Fit decides where you go. Belonging supports who you are becoming.

Designing for career belonging requires shifting from individual adaptation to systemic responsibility. Hiring, performance reviews, promotion logic, and AI tools must begin from the assumption that professionals are complex and interconnected wholes, not isolated traits to be picked apart and sorted.

The shift from fit to belonging is foundational because it changes the purpose of workforce systems. It replaces categorization with understanding. Until we design for career belonging, we will continue treating the symptoms of misrecognition, while leaving the architecture that produces it intact.

Shift #2: From Sorting to Seeing

How might we rethink how systems perceive and interpret people in the first place?

Workforce systems sort because it allows institutions to process large numbers of people quickly. We use a number of data points to do this: Degrees for expertise, job titles for seniority and positional authority, skills lists for competencies, personality assessments for strengths, tendencies, and aptitudes, and resumes and CVs to summarize trajectories and chronologies of accomplishments.

Such tools help leaders and systems make decisions about where and how someone might fit and advance, but they are limited. For instance, a resume hardly explains why someone chose certain work experiences. A job title says little about how someone thinks, works, or integrates knowledge across boundaries. Even job interviews and performance reviews are contrived spaces where the interviewee says what they believe will help them, while managers listen for familiar terms and are unconsciously influenced by personalities and their own bias.

Seeing who someone is in their work is different from sorting.

Sorting asks, *"Which category does this person belong to?"*

Seeing asks, *"What pattern of contribution emerges from who this person is?"*

Seeing is interpretive. It looks beyond what's on paper and what can be codified. It seeks to understand invisible work that goes unnamed. It perceives uncategorizable elements of a person and makes connections between seemingly disparate attributes.

Seeing asks, *"What's the throughline? What's the common thread? Who is this person beyond the roles they have held?"* It pays attention to the spaces in between, it doesn't overlook them. In other words, seeing recognizes the complexity and distinctiveness of a person's professional identity in order to accurately value it.

Importantly, this is not simply a matter of individuals telling better career stories. In fact, the explosion of storytelling advice, personal branding frameworks, and resume strategies is partly a response to the problem of seeing. When systems cannot interpret professional identity accurately, or at all, the burden falls on individuals to translate themselves into language that those systems can understand. But this translation has limits. No amount of narrative refinement can fully solve a structural interpretation gap. People can explain themselves more clearly, but if the systems evaluating them still rely on categories and keywords, much of their identity will remain invisible.

That's why this shift is systemic.

Workforce infrastructure must evolve beyond sorting and develop interpretive frameworks capable of recognizing hidden value across work experiences and roles. This shift is becoming even more urgent as AI becomes embedded in workforce systems. Hiring platforms, talent marketplaces, and advancement tools are increasingly mediated by algorithms trained on historical hiring and promotion data. If those systems learn only the patterns of the past, they will replicate and accelerate the same logic that already narrows opportunity.

Algorithms are very good at identifying people who resemble what has already been recognized. They become far less capable of recognizing outliers and emergent forms of value that do not yet have a clear category.

This means the shift from sorting to seeing is both technical and philosophical. The problem is not that people cannot explain themselves, it's that our systems do not yet know how to understand them. To change that, we need new language, tools, frameworks, and mental models for how to talk about professional identity so we have shared understanding across sectors.

Shift #3: From Developing Talent to Developing Professional Identity

Workforce systems already have established practices for developing talent, but we do not yet have comparable practices for developing professional identity.

Developing talent is typically tied to performance and progression inside existing structures. It is part of professional growth plans that focus on strengthening competencies, closing leadership gaps, and preparing people for future roles or opportunities. Development plans are often organized around what someone lacks relative to an existing position: more executive presence, stronger data fluency, broader strategic thinking, stronger technical mastery. The underlying assumption is that advancement happens when a person becomes a better match for the next known category.

Developing professional identity is different because it begins with a different question. Instead of asking **what someone needs to do** in order to reach their next role, it asks whether we fully understand **who this person is** in their work, including the deeper pattern of value they bring that may not be captured by their title, job description, or formal responsibilities.

When professional identity becomes part of workforce systems, people are asked how they understand themselves and their contribution beyond title alone. Doing so looks like this: One person may describe themselves as a polisher of diamonds in the rough who takes unfinished work and makes it ready to present. Another may identify as an opportunity translator, someone who consistently notices hidden openings between people, ideas, and partners and moves them forward. Another may share that although their title says operations director, much of their contribution comes from being a pattern stabilizer in moments of complexity.

These answers reveal deeper truths about who a person is and how they create value. With the inclusion of identity language, career conversations can connect performance with meaning instead of treating them as separate domains. Advancement becomes informed not only by what someone has done, but by the kind of contribution they are uniquely positioned to make because of their professional identity.

Conversations shift from "How do we develop you based on your goals?" to "How do you see yourself in your work, and how do we support the growth of that professional identity?"

This also changes what managers are trained to notice. During a performance review, for example, a manager may look beyond completed deliverables and recognize that one employee consistently brings unusual synthesis across conversations, anticipates downstream consequences others miss, or creates trust across functions where others struggle. These qualities often influence important decisions, yet they rarely appear in competency rubrics because they do not fit standard performance language. Instead of remaining informal observations, identity-based insights should become part of how hiring, development, performance, and advancement are understood.

Without identity-based tools embedded into talent systems, this becomes a hidden cost. We continue developing what is easiest to measure while overlooking what may be most distinctive. To change that, we need shared methodologies for interpreting how people want to be seen, known, and valued in their work. That means training leaders, managers, HR professionals, people-development teams, and career advisors to recognize professional identity, building more comprehensive recognition systems for identity-based sensemaking, and creating frameworks that capture the fuller picture of someone's value.

It also means reducing our reliance on matching, profiling, and sorting as the dominant logic of workforce decision-making, while intentionally training AI and emerging technologies to recognize hybridity and multi-dimensionality rather than filtering them out.

What Needs to Be on Our Radar

These shifts will not happen all at once. Some are already underway, some are emerging, and others may take years before they become visible as new norms. Here's an overview of how these shifts might unfold in the years to come.

Now

AI is already amplifying the limits of existing workforce categories. Applicants are using AI to write resumes while employers increasingly rely on AI to read, rank, and filter them, creating a strange loop where both sides generate and assess language optimized for systems rather than meaning. At the same time, competency-based hiring continues compressing identity into keywords, even as hybrid and multi-hyphenate professionals are growing faster than job architecture can meaningfully interpret. We are entering a period where workforce systems are becoming more efficient at processing people while often becoming less capable of understanding them.

Soon

Longer careerspans mean more people will move through multiple careers, portfolio-based work, and fluid contribution models shaped by projects rather than permanent roles, reflecting what longevity researchers have already begun to describe as the logic of the hundred-year life. Internal talent marketplaces will continue growing, but without stronger interpretive frameworks they may simply reorganize opportunity using the same narrow signals already embedded in hiring and promotion systems.

Later

The deeper shifts ahead are toward identity-first workforce development and career systems. This means professional identity becoming a recognized layer of workforce infrastructure, informing how people are educated, developed, advanced, and understood across sectors. Contribution may increasingly be valued not only by role or title, but by the distinct pattern of value a person creates across contexts, making hybrid identities and hybridized career tracks more normal than exceptional. Over time, professional identity development may emerge as its own cross-sector field, shaping the language, tools, and systems that sit beneath modern careers.

None of this will happen by accident, which is why the future of work needs clearer design principles for building career belonging into systems.

Ten Design Principles for Career Belonging

If career belonging is to be embedded in the future of work, it must be included in the design of those systems. Here's how we can do that:

1. *Professional identity is the foundation of career belonging.*

Professional identity sits upstream of workforce systems. It informs how people are represented in their resumes, narratives, and roles. Career belonging emerges from how clearly someone understands who they are in their work and how accurately they are seen, known, and valued by others. Hiring, development, and advancement decisions should be grounded in an understanding of who someone is, not just what they can do.

2. Every individual holds a unique professional identity and distinct value.

Standardization and mass categorization often fail to interpret multidimensional and hybrid professional identities, reducing or misunderstanding someone's value. More nuanced ways of recognizing unconventional experiences, capabilities, and contributions are required.

3. Development must extend beyond "talent" to include professional identity.

Growth is not only about building skills and knowledge, but about clarifying, articulating, and evolving who someone is and is becoming in their work.

4. Being seen, known, and valued must be intentionally taught and practiced.

These are not passive outcomes, they are skills. Individuals and systems alike must learn how to accurately see, deeply understand, and appropriately value someone the way they want to be seen.

5. Both Big C Careers and little c careers must be accounted for.

Titles, roles, and measurable achievements are only part of the picture. A person's broader constellation of work experiences in conjunction with their professional identity must inform career conversations and decisions.

6. Advocacy for professional identity must be supported and expected.

Individuals should be able to name and express who they are in their work beyond roles, and that information must be integrated into workforce systems.

7. Contrast sharpens belonging.

Moments of friction, misalignment, and misrecognition provide essential data for clarifying where identity is misunderstood and refining direction.

8. Reflection and sensemaking are essential to accurate interpretation.

Understanding professional identity requires both internal reflection and external perspective, making feedback and sensemaking frameworks critical. Other people often see patterns we cannot yet name in ourselves.

9. Career belonging exists across three levels: self, others, and something greater.

A career belongs to the individual, is reflected by others, and is part of something greater, such as a broader system, group or purpose. All three levels matter.

10. Systems can support career belonging, but cannot define it.

Employers, educators, managers, and technologies influence career belonging, but they do not determine it. No structure, role, technology or institution has the authority to determine who someone is in their work and what their big C Career means to them, but systems can be useful in aiding better reflection and sensemaking.

These principles provide guidance on how we move beyond outdated models of career fit toward systems that can actually interpret and support modern workers with multidimensional professional identities.

The Future Is a Question of Who and What We Choose to See

As society adapts to the realities of longer lives and longer careers, we must accept that unpredictability, reinvention, and new forms of work are becoming ordinary features of modern professional life.

According to the Foundation for Young Australians, the average young person today is expected to hold seventeen different jobs across five industries over the course of their working life. The number of transitions most people experience will continue to grow, making adaptability, reflection, and self-reinvention essential features—not bugs—of navigating work in the decades ahead.

We must imagine a future where career belonging is a priority. A future where people are not scared of being themselves or forced to reduce themselves into job titles, narrow narratives, and predefined categories simply to be employable.

Over time, career fit will feel increasingly insufficient because it cannot hold the complexity, fluidity, and multidimensionality that modern careers now require. To prepare for what is ahead, we need new ways of seeing, developing, and valuing people so that work evolves without losing sight of who people actually are within it.

Next Steps

- **Reflect**: Where have workforce systems in your career failed to fully see, understand, or value your professional identity, and how would you begin to reshape those systems?

- **Define**: Referring to the ten design principles of career belonging, which ones are you most ready to apply right away, and what might that look like in practice? Which ones feel necessary but harder to apply and why?

- **Do**: Make one shift in how you show up in your work going forward—whether in how you position yourself, evaluate others, or make career decisions— that prioritizes seeing and valuing professional identity over sorting for fit.

DEEPER CONVERSATIONS FOR SPECIFIC AUDIENCES

Gen Z and Career Belonging

Gen Z, the generation born between the mid-1990s and early 2010s, is redefining work, success, and belonging. Unlike previous generations, they view their careers not just as a means to earn a living but as an extension of their identity and values. For them, authenticity and purpose are paramount, shaping their decisions about where they work and what they do. Understanding their unique needs and perspectives is crucial for building workplaces where they can thrive.

In the book *Gen Z, Explained*, author Roberta Katz noted, "Gen Z are crafting entirely new identities that are highly individualized. They're unbundling and remixing with an imperative to self define."

To explore this phenomenon and its connection to career belonging, I spoke with Dr. Corey Seemiller, a sociologist, educator, and leading expert on Gen Z. Dr. Seemiller is the co-author of *Generation Z: A Century in the Making* and the recently released *Generations in the World of Work*. Her TED Talk on how Gen Z plans to make a difference has garnered more than a quarter-million views, and her work has been featured in *The New York Times, Time Magazine, USA Today,* and more. She has conducted one of the largest Gen Z studies, surveying over 30,000 participants across 81 countries, with findings published in her book, Gen Z Around the World.

Dr. Seemiller's extensive research and experience working with young adults have made her a trusted authority on the characteristics, motivations, and challenges of this dynamic generation. During our conversation, she shared invaluable insights into what Gen Z seeks in their careers, the obstacles they encounter, and how managers and organizations can better support them.

Interview with Dr. Corey Seemiller

Q1: How does Gen Z define success in their careers compared to other generations?

Dr. Seemiller: Gen Z's idea of success is closely tied to purpose, meaningfulness, and happiness. When we asked them to describe their ideal career, many emphasized intrinsic values like fulfillment and making a difference. Interestingly, money was not a central focus. When it did come up, it was about having "enough to live off of" rather than accumulating wealth. Their approach is more about finding a sense of calling and doing work that aligns with their values rather than simply achieving financial milestones.

Q2: What role do authenticity and individuality play in how Gen Z approaches work?

Dr. Seemiller: Authenticity is a non-negotiable for Gen Z. They want to bring their whole selves to work, and this includes being addressed by their preferred pronouns, dressing in ways that feel authentic to them, and working in inclusive environments. A commitment to diversity, equity, and inclusion (DEI) is particularly important to them. In fact, many Gen Zers see a company's DEI initiatives as a signal that the workplace will value their individuality and make space for others to do the same. This emphasis on authenticity is also tied to their desire for work that feels purpose-driven and aligned with their personal values.

Q3: How does Gen Z view career paths, and how is this different from traditional models?

Dr. Seemiller: Gen Z is transforming the traditional idea of career paths. Many are rejecting the old "go to school, get a degree, climb the ladder" model. They're skeptical of accumulating debt for college unless they're certain about their career goals. Some are opting for vocational training, freelancing, or side hustles, allowing them to explore their interests while maintaining financial flexibility. We've even seen Gen Z being dubbed the "Toolkit Generation" because of their focus on acquiring practical, transferable skills. However, there is still limited longitudinal data on how their career paths might evolve over time.

Q4: What does career belonging mean to Gen Z, and how does it relate to being seen, known, and valued?

Dr. Seemiller: For Gen Z, this generation is looking for workplaces where their contributions matter and where they can express their unique identities. That said, what we know about Gen Z and career belonging comes from broad research on their values, as data on belonging, specifically, isn't as prevalent in the literature.

Q5: What challenges do Gen Z face in achieving career belonging in traditional work structures?

Dr. Seemiller: Traditional workplaces often emphasize conformity and hierarchical structures, which can clash with Gen Z's desire for authenticity and innovation. Economic challenges also play a significant role. Many Gen Zers are juggling side hustles or taking jobs outside their preferred fields to make ends meet. These pressures can make it difficult to find work that aligns with their values and fosters a sense of career belonging. While we have some research on this, more studies are needed to fully understand the unique barriers related to career belonging they face in traditional work settings.

Q6: How can employers and managers support Gen Z in achieving career belonging?

Dr. Seemiller: One of the most effective strategies is fostering meaningful mentoring relationships. Gen Z values mentoring that is reciprocal—where they can both teach and learn. Cross-generational mentoring and intergenerational mentoring triads, where individuals of different ages exchange perspectives, are particularly effective. Employers should also lean into DEI efforts and prioritize well-being initiatives. These steps signal to Gen Z that they're valued as individuals and not just as employees.

Q7: Are there practical tools or strategies that resonate with Gen Z for career planning?

Dr. Seemiller: Gen Z is drawn to DIY learning and development tools. They often turn to TED Talks, YouTube, and even TikTok for career advice and professional growth. They're less likely to attend traditional conferences unless they can go with a group of peers. Instead, they prefer accessible, digital resources that allow them to learn on their own terms. While these preferences are clear, it will be interesting to see how these habits impact long-term career outcomes.

For more information and resources on Gen Z by Dr. Seemiller:

- www.coreyseemiller.com
- TEDx: Generation Z: Making a Difference Their Way

Gifted Adults and Career Belonging

When I reflect on the individuals who have sought my guidance on professional identity and career belonging, I estimate that nearly half have been gifted adults. I recognize this because I am one too.

Gifted adults represent a unique segment of the workforce, characterized by exceptional abilities, intense emotions, and an insatiable curiosity. These traits often set them apart—fueling extraordinary achievements while also posing challenges when navigating traditional career paths. Although gifted individuals frequently excel in specific areas, their pursuit of depth, meaning, and alignment can conflict with rigid workplace norms and expectations.

The concept of career belonging offers a transformative framework for addressing these challenges. Unlike career fit—which encourages individuals to conform to predefined roles—career belonging emphasizes seeing, knowing, and valuing yourself in your work while also understanding how this identity is reflected by others and something greater than yourself. It also involves advocating for yourself so that others can understand and appreciate your career as you do.

For gifted adults, this shift is particularly significant. Career fit often requires masking multifaceted identities, while career belonging creates a space to embrace and express complexity without fear of judgment or exclusion.

Many gifted adults wrestle with feelings of being "too much" or "not enough" in the workplace and in the workforce. They possess tremendous assets—such as intensity, strong moral convictions, and insatiable curiosity—yet these traits are often misunderstood or undervalued by peers and supervisors. Their multipotentiality—the ability to thrive across multiple domains—can also make it challenging to define a singular career path. In a professional world increasingly focused on specialization, gifted adults often feel pressured to narrow their identities to fit conventional molds, sacrificing authenticity and fulfillment.

Compounding these challenges, many gifted adults strive for self-actualization through their work—seeking not just a career but a calling. Maslow emphasized that true self-actualization involves contributing to something greater than oneself, a fundamental pillar of career belonging. As Maslow observed, "What [self-actualizing people] do is very conscious of being useful to others and humanity. There is nothing self-serving, absorbing, or solely about seeking personal fulfillment. Fulfillment exists within a broader, more expansive frame."

Noted scholar Dr. Deborah Ruf makes an important distinction between career self-actualization and inner self-actualization. In her view, career self-actualization involves achieving success within a professional context, but it doesn't necessarily involve personal growth. Inner self-actualization, on the other hand, demands deep personal transformation. Dr. Ruf explains:

> Career self-actualization refers to finding success in your career by becoming a responsible, contributing member of society, but it lacks the identity development and inner transformation aspect. Inner self-actualization refers to people who have undergone one or more significant developmental crises in their lives and, from that inner growth, have found a new complexity of understanding and a richer view of the world. Undergoing inner self-transformation does not mean someone is successful in their career; they may or may not have career and financial success.

Achieving career belonging often involves identity development—particularly redefining professional identities. For gifted adults, this process can encompass both career and inner self-actualization, as the interplay between self-awareness and career success is essential to their sense of belonging.

Given strong interest I've received from gifted adults seeking this guidance, I felt it was essential to dedicate a chapter to exploring how their approach to career belonging differs from others. To offer deeper insights into this topic, I invited Dr. Joi Lin to share her expertise.

Dr. Lin is a leading voice in giftedness. As a scholar and practitioner with a profound understanding of the challenges gifted individuals face, Dr. Lin offers a valuable perspective on career development within the gifted population. She is an expert in gifted education and holds a master's degree in industrial and organizational psychology.

Following is a conversation I had with Dr. Lin about gifted adults and career belonging. With her thoughtful and practical wisdom, she sheds light on how gifted individuals experience career belonging and the unique approaches needed to help them align their diverse abilities. By understanding the distinct ways gifted adults operate in the workplace, both individuals and organizations can create environments where these exceptional talents can thrive and feel a sense of belonging.

If you're not sure whether you're a gifted adult, a good starting point is Dr. Linda Silverman's *Giftedness in Adults Rating Scale*. This 25-question self-assessment prompts you to rate yourself on questions such as, "Are you a good problem solver?" "Do you have good long-term memory?" and "Do you have an extraordinary sense of humor?" The link to this resource is in the appendix.

Interview with Dr. Joi Lin

Question: How do the experiences of gifted adults in the workplace differ from those of others, particularly regarding their ability to feel seen, known, and valued?

Dr. Joi Lin: Gifted adults often find themselves in workplaces that lack an understanding of their unique traits. Many workplaces aren't equipped to recognize the nuances of giftedness, let alone harness or celebrate it. This often leaves gifted individuals feeling only partially seen—acknowledged perhaps for their high performance but not valued as whole, multidimensional people.

For example, they may excel in a particular role and receive recognition for their output, but that acknowledgment rarely extends to their broader capacities or their need for intellectual and emotional depth. This can create a paradox where their work is valued, but they as individuals are not. Gifted adults frequently experience social anxiety and exclusion, as their intensities and emotional depth may not align with workplace norms. They may thrive in environments that appreciate high creativity or moral passion, but feel stifled in settings that demand conformity or superficial social engagement.

Many gifted people are also twice-exceptional or multi-exceptional with additional learning or physical disabilities. Gifted people with ADHD, autism, sensory processing issues, etc. may experience additional frustrations in the workplace and require additional accommodations to thrive.

Question: In your experience, how does the concept of "fit" manifest for gifted individuals, and how might it fail them compared to the idea of belonging?

Dr. Joi Lin: The idea of "fit" often feels like trying to squeeze into a mold that's too small. Fit suggests a perfect alignment, like a puzzle piece snapping into place. For gifted individuals, this is almost never the case. They have too many edges, too many facets to their identities. Realistically, the spaces gifted people inhabit must be expansive enough to accommodate their multidimensional nature.

A particularly apt metaphor is an online video that shows a 3D puzzle box where the goal is to push each block through its corresponding hole. The person in the video shows that all shapes can actually fit through the square hole—because the square hole is big enough for each of them to fit. It's not a precise fit, but it works. For gifted adults, the workplace "fit" must function similarly—it needs flexibility and breadth. Unfortunately, many workplaces expect individuals to conform to rigid expectations, which often requires gifted adults to mask parts of themselves. This constant effort to conform can lead to burnout and a diminished sense of belonging. Belonging, by contrast, emphasizes a space where all parts of a person—quirks, strengths, and even flaws—are accepted.

Question: How does multipotentiality or hybrid professional identity impact their ability to find career belonging?

Dr. Joi Lin: Multipotentiality—the ability to excel in multiple fields—adds both richness and complexity to a gifted adult's career journey. These individuals often feel pulled in several directions, as their interests and talents span diverse domains. While this creates opportunities for innovative and hybrid career paths, it can also lead to a lack of clarity or focus. Multipotentiality can also foster a fear of premature foreclosure–the idea that making any choice limits other choices which can lead to the procrastination of career decisions.

What makes multipotentiality challenging is that society rewards specialization. Gifted adults frequently feel pressured to narrow their scope, which can be stifling. Some gifted individuals thrive in roles that allow them to wear multiple hats, such as working in startups or creating their own entrepreneurial ventures. However, the challenge lies in communicating the value of their hybridity in a workforce that often struggles to understand it.

Question: Gifted individuals often report feeling "out of place" in traditional work settings. How might this impact their mental health and ability to sustain a fulfilling career?

Dr. Joi Lin: Feeling out of place can take a significant toll on mental health. Gifted individuals who do not feel valued or seen often internalize this disconnect, leading to frustration, stress, and even depression. The workplace can feel isolating when their unique traits—such as moral intensity or deep curiosity—aren't understood or appreciated.

This misalignment not only impacts their mental health but also makes it difficult to sustain a fulfilling career. When gifted individuals are forced to suppress their authentic selves or over-perform to gain recognition, they risk burnout. Creating environments where gifted adults can thrive requires a cultural shift toward inclusion and appreciation of diverse ways of thinking.

Question: Are there specific tools or exercises you recommend for gifted adults to discover their core truths and align their careers with their identities and values?

Dr. Joi Lin: One of the most important tools is intentional self-reflection. Gifted adults should take time to explore their core passions and values. Journaling, mentorship, and even structured assessments can help illuminate their unique strengths and aspirations. Networking is also critical—finding like-minded individuals in their field can provide validation and opportunities.

I often advise gifted individuals to research their field and identify thought leaders whose work resonates with their interests. By studying these role models and reaching out for conversations or mentorship, gifted adults can better align their career paths with their authentic selves.

HR Professionals, Managers, and Career Belonging

HR professionals and managers play a vital role in shaping how employees experience career belonging. Traditionally, HR practices have focused on finding the "right fit"—matching individuals to predefined roles based on skills, competencies, and organizational needs. But as the nature of work evolves, so must the way we think about career growth. Employees today are not just seeking roles that align with their qualifications. Instead, they want to feel seen, known, and valued in their work.

To explore this shift, I spoke with Julie Winkle Giulioni— a globally recognized expert in career development and leadership growth. Julie has spent her career championing workplace development. She is the co-author of the international bestseller *Help Them Grow or Watch Them Go,* and author of *Promotions Are So Yesterday.* She consults with organizations worldwide, offering speaking and training services designed to develop their most sustainable competitive advantage: their people. Known for her fresh, inspiring, and actionable leadership strategies, Julie is the ideal expert to discuss how HR can move beyond traditional career fit to foster true career belonging.

I admire how Julie challenges the fields of career and professional development to adopt a more expansive, multidimensional approach. Contemporary career development is no longer just about promotions or climbing the corporate ladder; as Julie puts it, it's about "countless moments that come together to create rich, fulfilling careers." In *Promotions Are So Yesterday*, she emphasizes the importance of "expanding [our] definitions of careers to include all that can be developed and grown throughout one's life at work."

One of Julie's key insights from our interview is that embedding career belonging into organizational life requires a compelling business case—something HR professionals are uniquely positioned to develop and promote. Once executives and leaders recognize the role career belonging plays in driving engagement, productivity, innovation, retention, and future-proofing the workforce, it becomes an obvious priority. Employees who experience career belonging—not just a good fit—are more likely to stay, contribute effectively, and feel genuinely connected to organizational outcomes and performance. Career belonging can't be treated as a "feel good" initiative. It must become a strategic imperative, and HR can make it happen.

Interview with Julie Winkle Giulioni

Question: What are your thoughts on the difference between career fit and career belonging, especially from an HR perspective?

Julie Winkle Giulioni: Until now career fit has been the standard approach. Employees are assigned predefined roles much like putting the right piece in a jigsaw puzzle or painting-by-numbers on a pre-drawn picture. It's typically a structured, transactional approach where HR and hiring managers try to drop the right color on the right spot on the canvas to help their organizations maintain order. But 'fit' is static—it assumes that both the job and the employee remain the same over time. And there's an inherently external orientation.

Career belonging, on the other hand, is more of an inside job. It involves dynamic emotional and psychological connection. It reflects an employee's evolving sense of self-awareness, purpose, and how they integrate their work into their identity. This makes people feel authentically valued, integral to the work they're doing, and meaningfully connected to the organization's success.

This fresh approach of career belonging offers HR professionals and others a richer and more varied palette with which to paint. It allows us to paint outside of the lines, in the margins and all over the canvas with colors that are unique to the individual. And as a reflection of this process, career belonging promotes the innovation and agility that's required in today's quickly evolving world.

Savvy HR professionals will see that career belonging really drives the profound employee experience and connection that leads to stronger retention, engagement, and innovation that's so important to organizations. Career belonging puts the 'human' back in human resources at a time when many HR professionals and organizations are looking to amplify that kind of humanity.

Question: Why might HR managers and talent developers resist moving away from the idea of career fit?

Julie Winkle Giulioni: First, I anticipate that the ideas in this book are going to spark a lot of enthusiasm, curiosity, and interest in HR professionals who are looking for ways to elevate the employee experience and distinguish their organizations in a competitive environment. But, let's face it, change is hard. And there are a few typical sources of resistance–comfort and tradition being the main ones. Career fit has been the dominant approach for decades. It feels measurable and easy to manage. Fit also aligns with existing HR structures like competency-based hiring and performance evaluations.

The idea of career belonging introduces ambiguity; it feels less tangible and perhaps harder to operationalize. Career belonging runs counter to work that may be underway around skills and competency-based hiring. Some folks in HR and talent acquisition may feel tension in squaring these two ideas. Squaring a 'skills first' approach with career belonging will take some time, thought, and discussion by HR, talent acquisition, and others in the organization.

Question: What strategies can HR managers use to help employees feel seen, known, and valued in their roles?

Julie Winkle Giulioni: HR can't do this alone—as they say, it takes a village. HR can lead the way, but they must train and enable leaders to take the day-to-day actions that support career belonging.

One of the most powerful tools that supports career belonging is the career conversation. Unfortunately, leaders typically need help and support to make it happen—which is where HR can step in. Leaders need to understand that these conversations can't just be annual performance reviews, but regular discussions about an employee's aspirations, interests, skills, and evolving sense of self. This creates trust and rapport that builds the kinds of relationships required for sustainable belonging, career and otherwise.

Leaders also need to be trained to recognize and engage with employees beyond their job descriptions. Offering leaders tools and strategies to talk to people about their career is huge. Leaders need models of what this looks like and need to be coached on how to create feedback loops.

Finally, at an organizational level, we tend to celebrate promotions and formal achievements, but we need to learn how to embrace and practice recognition beyond roles - whether it's growth in new skills, mentorship, innovation, or even developing a greater sense of self awareness. What gets recognized at an organizational level is perceived as important and gets repeated, creating virtuous cycles that acknowledge and elevate career belonging.

Question: In your book Promotions Are So Yesterday, you emphasize alternatives to upward mobility. How does this philosophy connect with career belonging?

Julie Winkle Giulioni: I see so many synergies here. It all begins with an employee's understanding of their interests and the relationship they want to have with their work and with their growth. My multidimensional career framework and your career belonging model both offer authentic ways for people to express themselves and their evolving selves within the context of their careers. My set of alternative dimensions beyond promotions primes the pump for those looking for a greater level of career belonging.

I think it's worth noting that career belonging thrives within the broader definition of career development. Employees need to see diverse opportunities to grow without being confined to a ladder or traditional roles. Alternatives to promotions like skill-building, rotations, projects, any number of experiences that drive engagement and growth and emphasize intrinsic value are central to your definition of career belonging.

Question: What role does organizational culture play in fostering career belonging?

Julie Winkle Giulioni: Culture is everything. It doesn't just influence how people feel about their employer— it shapes how they feel about themselves within the organization. A culture that fosters career belonging is going to value, model and recognize things like reflection, growth, adaptability, self-awareness, exploration, and the list goes on.

HR professionals can take the lead in creating this kind of culture by generating support with senior leadership, helping them understand the value by building the business case for this. That's key. Since we can link career belonging to important outcomes like engagement, productivity, innovation, retention, and more, HR can directly address the things that are keeping senior leaders up at night.

Question: What advice would you give HR leaders who want to implement career belonging practices but don't know where to start?

Julie Winkle Giulioni: Instead of rigid containers that box people in, we need to think in terms of clear, translucent, see-through, semi-permeable containers that allow us to hold space for necessary hard skills and competencies, but also allow other dimensions of a person to show through. People still need to do the specifics associated with their jobs, but this approach allows the space for other parts–and the whole person–to be recognized in a more organic and expansive way.

If HR is interested in cultivating this sort of culture, it might be wise to begin with listening tours—talking to employees to understand their perceptions of career growth and belonging. And remember that small wins matter—launch isolated pilots and see some successes before rolling out large-scale initiatives.

The learning and development function within organizations can be really helpful too. The role of reflection and self-awareness are so central to career belonging, but it's becoming a dying art. It's not something a lot of us carve out time for, so how do we embed more? Reflection should be part of all learning efforts.

Finally, rich questions about career belonging should be embedded in performance reviews, succession planning, interviews, and the onboarding process. That could look like asking questions about how well employees feel seen, known, and valued for who they are besides their skills and job titles.

Question: How do you see career belonging evolving with the rise of Gen Z and hybrid work models?

Julie Winkle Giulioni: Gen Z is the perfect group to move career belonging forward into the workplace because they demand authenticity and nonbinary structures. They expect work to align with their personal values and reject rigid career boxes. They're also forcing organizations to have more transparent and purpose-driven conversations about career development. I think this generation demands what so many of us in other generations have wanted but haven't felt comfortable demanding. So Gen Z will pave the way for us all.

In terms of hybrid work, it introduces both opportunities and challenges for career belonging. On one hand, it gives employees more control over their work-life balance, which gives them a greater chance to explore the nature of their career belonging. While conducting research to write the new edition of *Help Them Grow*, we learned about the indispensable role of intentionality in remote and hybrid environments. Leaders must proactively create virtual spaces, amplify communication, make visible what's not seen, and deliberately engineer growth opportunities for all. Intentionality is key to ensuring career belonging is happening.

Question: What new challenges or opportunities do you anticipate HR professionals and managers will face in the next decade when addressing career belonging?

Julie Winkle Giulioni: HR will need to navigate:

- Balancing upskilling with career belonging—helping employees future-proof their careers and continue evolving without reducing them to a set of competencies.
- The human vs. tech balance—ensuring that AI-driven hiring and skills assessments don't overshadow the holistic human aspects of career growth.
- The rise of the gig economy—figuring out how to foster career belonging for contract workers and freelancers who aren't tied to a single employer. How do they feel seen, known, and valued when they're a "hired hand"?

At its core, career belonging is about helping employees be seen in their work—not just as job titles, but as evolving professionals who contribute in ways that matter to them, their organizations, their customers, and to something bigger than themselves. HR professionals who embrace this mindset will future proof their organizations by fostering a workforce that is engaged, adaptable, and deeply connected to their careers—and in the process will deliver unbeatable value to their organizations.

For more resources by Julie Winkle Giulioni:

- www.juliewinklegiulioni.com
- Books : *Help Them Grow or Watch Them Go* and *Promotions are SO Yesterday*

APPENDIX

More Support on Your Career Belonging Journey

If you're craving deeper clarity about your professional identity, or want more guidance as you move from career fit to career belonging, I've created a suite of powerful tools to help you along the way.

Visit **morethanmytitle.com** to access a growing library of resources designed to support you in feeling seen, known, and valued in your career.

You'll find:

- **Free AI Companion to this Book**
  An AI-powered self-reflection tool that helps you discover your *state of career being*, your *career persona*, and how they shape the way you show up in your work. You'll be pushed to answer: *"How clearly do you understand who you are in your career right now?"*

- **Free Workbooks & Guides**
  Downloadable exercises and tools that align with the frameworks in this book, including the Career

Belonging Matrix, SKV reflection prompts, and more.

 morethanmytitle.com

Resources for Crossing Your Career Chasm

Books

- *The War of Art: Break Through the Blocks and Win Your Inner Creative Battles* by Steven Pressfield

- *The Crossroads of Should and Must: Find and Follow Your Passion* by Elle Luna

- *How We Heal: Uncover Your Power and Set Yourself Free* by Alexandra Elle

- *The Artist's Way: A Spiritual Path to Higher Creativity* by Julia Cameron

- *Draw Your Feelings: A Creative Journal to Help You Make Sense of Your Emotions* by Rukmini Poddar

- *From Strength to Strength: Finding Success, Happiness, and Deep Purpose in the Second Half of Life* by Arthur C. Brooks

- *Becoming You: Crafting the Authentic Career You've Always Wanted* by Suzy Welch

- *Working Identity: Unconventional Strategies for Reinventing Your Career* by Herminia Ibarra

- *Composing a Life* by Mary Catherine Bateson

Poetry

- *Maia Poetry* by Maia https://www.maiapoetry.com/

- *A Gentle Reminder* by Bianca Sparacino

Watch

- *In & of Itself* by Derek DelGaudio https://www.inandofitselfshow.com/ or https://www.imdb.com/title/tt11916302/

- *Increase Your Self-Awareness with One Simple Fix* by Dr. Tasha Eurich https://www.ted.com/talks/tasha_eurich_increase_your_self_awareness_with_one_simple_fix

- Yoann Bourgeois Captivates Audience with Powerful Performance About Life (Original Video) https://youtu.be/x_DA3dgRSrw?si=lzjiTmAkXreGHqKm

Examples of Being Seen, Known, and Valued (SKV's)

As you work through the Career Belonging Matrix, it's helpful to have a list of what it looks like to be seen, known, and valued in your career to use for inspiration.

Here are specific examples of little ways that aren't little at all. All of these can be tailored to fit the three levels of belonging:

- Respecting boundaries and commitments outside of work
- Timely and honest feedback
- Praise
- Gratitude
- Rituals
- Receiving a handwritten note
- Responding to work stress with grace and kindness
- Responding to work concerns with love and care
- Being empowered to make decisions
- Celebrating work wins and successes
- Telling work related stories that illustrate someone's impact

- Being transparent
- Taking a break without feeling guilty
- Open and honest communication
- Remembering favorite work related things, passions, and interests
- Eye contact
- Comfortable silence
- Sharing something together
- Kept promises
- Remembering small details or a work story you told
- The way someone says your name
- Reciprocity
- Liking the way you feel when you're around someone
- Being told "I'm proud of you"

SKVs and Professional Development Plans

A professional development plan can reflect SKVs. Use them to help identify learning opportunities, projects, and career goals that align with how you want to be seen, known, and valued in your work.

For example, if you want to be seen as an expert in your field, consider pursuing advanced certifications or presenting at industry conferences. If you want to be valued for your collaboration skills, seek out team-based projects where you can shine.

Try using a modified version of the Career Belonging Matrix to share with your manager and build your professional development plan.

	By You	By Others	By Something Greater
Being Seen			
Being Known			
Being Valued			

Dimensions of a Great Career

There's no right way to measure a great career, but there are dimensions and variables that are discussed and weighed in terms of importance. Decide which dimensions are most important to your big C Career and use the questions below to deepen your reflection and definition of it.

Personal Growth Dimension	Work/Life Balance Dimension	Skill Dimension
• Do you find it challenging? • Do you find it rewarding? • Are you able to learn new things? • Are you growing? • Does it meet your values? • Are you proud of it? • Do you want to do it?	• Does it take the right amount of your time? Or too much time? • Is it sustainable or will it burn you out? • Does it invigorate you and give you energy? • Does it provide enough flexibility to meet your needs?	• Are you competent at it? • How much time will it take to become competent at it? • Can you continue to grow or evolve in it? • Will it challenge you over time?

Purpose/ Satisfaction Dimension	Education Dimension	Impact Dimension
• How happy are you in your work? • Are you fulfilling your purpose? • Is it your calling? • Are you fulfilling your potential?	• How much, if any, education do you need? • How long will it take to gain the required training?	• Are you doing good/ making positive change in the world? • Are you making a difference or leaving a legacy? • Are you solving an important problem?
Social/ Cultural Dimension:	**Financial Stability Dimension**	**Market Dimension**
• Do your friends and family support it? • Is it culturally or socially important or acceptable? • How much will depend on your individual ability versus social connections? • Is it hard to break into or become an expert in? • Are there many barriers, biases, or prejudices to navigate? • Is it growing, dying or emerging?	• Does it pay enough to meet or exceed your lifestyle needs? • Does it provide quality benefits?	• Does it feel secure/ stable? • Does the job market value it? • Does the world need it? • Is there demand? • Is it competitive, or hard to get into? • Will it be relevant in the next five, ten, twenty years from now?

Giftedness in Adults
Rating Scale

Silverman, Linda K. *Giftedness in Adults Rating Scale.* Denver, CO: Gifted Development Center, 2005.

https://static1.squarespace.com/static/5ec9e1a3d3815c7eb cd0503a/t/5f037adba2bbeb0eb1ab607f/1594063580259/ Giftedness+in+Adults+rating+scale+with+intro.pdf.

Glossary of Terms

Authentic Professional Identity: A clear understanding and expression of who you are in your work, combining your skills, values, beliefs, and unique talents.

Belonging: Being accepted for who you are, no matter what.

Big C Career: The constellation of meaningful events and experiences over your lifetime that you consider part of your work, akin to an oeuvre or body of work. It reflects a curated selection of impactful and purposeful activities rather than a mere chronological job history.

Calling: A transcendent summons to approach a particular life role, often characterized by finding meaning and purpose in work, which becomes inseparable from one's identity and purpose.

Career: The constellation of meaningful events and experiences over your lifetime that you consider to be part of your work (like an oeuvre, opus, or body of work). It often only makes sense in retrospect. Also see definitions for little c and big C Career.

Career Belonging: Being seen, known, and valued by yourself, others, and something bigger than yourself.

Career Chasm: The gap between your evolved professional identity and how it is currently recognized by career and workforce systems, often experienced as a delay between your little c and Big C Career.

Career Embodiment: Living in alignment with your professional identity and integrating your values, skills, and experiences into how you express yourself and make career choices.

Career Fight: Actively resisting or challenging obstacles and conventions that restrict your career growth, often marked by a determined effort to create opportunities.

Career Fit: The state of aligning your skills, qualifications, and experiences with the external demands of a job or role. Career fit focuses on meeting predefined expectations and external validation, often at the cost of suppressing parts of your authentic self.

Career Flight: A state of autonomy and deep self-knowledge where you step away from traditional career paths to align your values with work experiences. It signifies a liberation from rigid structures.

Career Freeze: Feeling stuck or paralyzed in your career, unable to move forward due to fear, uncertainty, or external barriers.

Career Fright: A fear-based reaction to career-related uncertainty, challenges, or transitions, often resulting in hesitation, anxiety, or avoidance of decision-making.

Career Pathing: A structured approach to defining and following a clear trajectory in your career, with recognizable milestones and goals.

Career Pathlessness: A state of not adhering to a predefined career path, embracing the ambiguity and freedom to explore varied opportunities.

Career Power Questions (CPQs): The foundational questions you must ask yourself to achieve career clarity: "Who are you in your work?", "What does that mean?", and "How do you want to be seen, known, and valued in your career?".

Dimensions of Belonging: The three key aspects of belonging: being seen, known, and valued by yourself, others, and something bigger than yourself.

Fit Versus Belonging: The distinction between molding yourself to match external job expectations (fit) and finding alignment where your authentic self is seen, known, and valued (belonging).

Gifted Adults: Individuals with exceptional abilities and intellectual capacity who often face challenges in fitting into traditional career structures because of their multi-dimensionality.

Hybrid Professional: A person who integrates multiple professional identities, working from the intersections of those identities, and who defies categorization.

Hybrid Professional Identity Integration: The process of blending multiple professional identities into a cohesive whole that is often interdisciplinary.

Job: A specific role or position held by an individual, typically focused on tasks and responsibilities within a particular organization. A job may be part of a career, but does not define the entirety of one's professional identity or purpose.

Known: Feeling recognized for the specific talents, experiences, and contributions you bring to your work. Being known involves understanding how others perceive and acknowledge your unique value.

Little c career: An occupation undertaken for a significant period of a person's life, often with opportunities for progress, aligns with traditional dictionary definitions.

Professional Identity: A noun that represents who you are and what you call yourself in your work (not your job title).

Professional Identity Crisis: When you lose your sense of yourself in your work and don't know who you are without a job title.

Seen: Feeling visible and acknowledged for your authentic professional identity and the multifaceted contributions you make in your work.

Self-Reflection: A critical practice in achieving career belonging, involving deep introspection to uncover your true professional identity and aspirations.

Valued: Feeling appreciated and respected for your contributions, talents, and unique identity. Being valued goes beyond skills to encompass recognition of your deeper significance and impact.

Work: Whatever you do for a living (in a moment of time), whether you get paid for it.

Workforce Systems: The structures and processes that organize work and determine how people are interpreted, evaluated, hired, developed, and advanced.

Workplace Belonging: Being accepted, valued, and supported for your unique contributions and identity within a professional setting.

Bibliography

80,000 Hours. "Start Here." Last modified December 2021. https://80000hours.org/start-here/?int_campaign=2021-12--primary-navigation__start-here.

Allen, Kelly-Ann, Dianne L. Gray, Roy F. Baumeister, and Mark R. Leary. "The Need to Belong: A Deep Dive into the Origins, Implications, and Future of a Foundational Construct." *Educational Psychology Review* 34, no. 2 (2022): 1133–1156. https://doi.org/10.1007/s10648-021-09633-6.

Antonsich, Marco. "Searching for Belonging: An Analytical Framework." *Geography Compass* 4, no. 6 (2010): 644–659. https://doi.org/10.1111/j.1749-8198.2009.00317.x.

Arthur, Michael B., and Denise M. Rousseau. *The Boundaryless Career: A New Employment Principle for a New Organizational Era.* Oxford: Oxford University Press, 1996.

Barringham, Nick, and Pam Barringham. *Finding People to Be There: Rebuilding a Sense of Belonging.* Brisbane, Australia: Anglicare, 2002.

Bateson, Mary Catherine. *Composing a Life.* New York: Grove Press, 2001.

Baumeister, Roy F., and Mark R. Leary. "The Need to Belong: Desire for Interpersonal Attachments as a Fundamental Human Motivation." *Psychological Bulletin* 117, no. 3 (1995): 497–529.

Berk, Sarabeth. *More Than My Title*. Chicago: Networlding Publishing, 2020.

Berger, John. *Ways of Seeing*. London: BBC and Penguin Books, 1972.

Bernard, Rachel E., and Emily H. G. Cooperdock. "No Progress on Diversity in 40 Years." *Nature Geoscience* 11 (2018): 292–295. https://doi.org/10.1038/s41561-018-0116-6.

BetterUp. *The Value of Belonging at Work: New Frontiers for Inclusion*. San Francisco: BetterUp, 2021. https://www.betterup.com/en-us/resources/articles/belonging-at-work.

Bloom, Matt, and Amy Colbert. "Stories of Calling: How Called Professionals Construct Narrative Identities." *Administrative Science Quarterly* 66, no. 2 (2020): 279–323. https://doi.org/10.1177/0001839220949502.

Brach, Tara. "Basic Trust – Part 1." *Tara Brach Podcast*, August 21, 2024. https://www.tarabrach.com/basic-trust-part-1_2024/.

Brach, Tara. "From Ego to Eco-Identity." Podcast episode, July 25, 2024. https://www.tarabrach.com/ego-to-eco-identity/.

Brown, Brené. *Atlas of the Heart: Mapping Meaningful Connection and the Language of Human Experience*. New York: Random House, 2021.

Brown, Brené. *Daring Greatly: How the Courage to Be Vulnerable Transforms the Way We Live, Love, Parent, and Lead*. New York: Penguin, 2015.

Burning Glass Technologies. *The Changing Nature of Work: How the Demand for Skills Has Shifted Over Time*. 2021. https://www.burning-glass.com/research-project/the-changing-nature-of-work/.

Cable, Daniel M., and Virginia S. Kay. "Striving for Self-Verification During Organizational Entry." *Academy of Management Journal* 55, no. 2 (2011): 360–380. https://doi.org/10.5465/amj.2010.0397.

Calmese, Dario. Interview by Debbie Millman. "Dario Calmese." *Design Matters*, February 13, 2023. https://www.designmattersmedia.com/podcast/2023/dario-calmese.

Campbell, Joseph. *The Hero's Journey: Joseph Campbell on His Life & Work*. Retrieved from https://www.goodreads.com/quotes/82893-you-enter-the-forest-at-the-darkest-point-where-there.

Cascio, Toni, and Janice Gasket. "Everyone Has a Shining Side: Computer-Mediated Mentoring in Social Work Education." *Journal of Social Work Education* 37, no. 2 (2001).

Clear, James. *Atomic Habits: An Easy & Proven Way to Build Good Habits & Break Bad Ones*. New York: Avery, 2018.

Cohen, Geoffrey. *Belonging: The Science of Creating Connection and Bridging Divides*. New York: Norton, 2022.

Cohen, Geoffrey L. "Understanding and Overcoming Belonging Uncertainty." *Behavioral Scientist*, October 10, 2022. https://behavioralscientist.org/understanding-and-overcoming-belonging-uncertainty/.

Crystal, Bethany. "Joining the Fractional Executive Movement." *Go Solo*, Medium, August 12, 2024. https://bethanymarz.medium.com/joining-the-fractional-executive-movement-b72a730ec573.

DataIntelo. "Online Career Test Market Report." https://dataintelo.com/report/global-online-career-test-market.

DelGaudio, Derek. *In & Of Itself*. Directed by Frank Oz. Hulu, 2021.

Elle, Alexandra. *How We Heal: Uncover Your Power and Set Yourself Free.* San Francisco: Chronicle Books, 2022. Also available at https://alexelle.substack.com/p/choosing-myself-at-35.

Elkins, James. *The Object Stares Back: On the Nature of Seeing.* New York: Simon & Schuster, 1996.

Eurich, Tasha. *Insight: The Surprising Truth About How Others See Us, How We See Ourselves, and Why the Answers Matter More Than We Think.* New York: Crown Currency, 2018.

Foundation for Young Australians. *The New Work Reality.* Melbourne: Foundation for Young Australians, 2018. https://www.fya.org.au/app/uploads/2021/09/TheNewWorkReality_2018.pdf.

Freire, Paulo. *Pedagogy of the Oppressed.* New York: Continuum, 1970.

Giulioni, Julie Winkle. *Help Them Grow or Watch Them Go: Career Conversations Organizations Need and Employees Want.* San Francisco: Berrett-Koehler Publishers, 2012.

Giulioni, Julie Winkle. *Promotions Are So Yesterday: Redefine Career Development. Help Employees Thrive.* Alexandria, VA: ATD Press, 2022.

Gkorezis, Panagiotis, and Stergios D. Daskalou. "The Role of Job Crafting in Employees' Psychological Capital and Workplace Belonging." *Current Psychology,* May 2023. https://link.springer.com/article/10.1007/s12144-023-04618-w.

Grant, Adam M. *Give and Take: A Revolutionary Approach to Success.* New York: Viking, 2013.

Harvard Business Review. "Your Career Doesn't Have to Have a Purpose." April 2024. https://hbr.org/2024/04/your-career-doesnt-need-to-have-a-purpose.

HRM Online. "Reconfiguring the Job Description for Dynamic Roles." *HRM Online Australia*. https://www.hrmonline.com.au/section/strategic-hr/reconfiguring-job-description-dynamic-roles/.

Ibarra, Herminia. *Working Identity: Unconventional Strategies for Reinventing Your Career.* Boston: Harvard Business School Press, 2003.

Innovius Research. "Career Counseling Market 2021–2030 Report." https://www.innoviusresearch.com/blog/market-report/career-counseling-market-2021-2030.

Jung, Carl Gustav. *Collected Works of C.G. Jung, Vol. 12: Psychology and Alchemy.* Translated by R. F. C. Hull. Princeton, NJ: Princeton University Press, 1968.

Kealey, Caroline. "Mic Drop from Esther Perel on Technology and Our Ability to Cope with Discomfort." *LinkedIn*, October 3, 2023. https://www.linkedin.com/pulse/mic-drop-esther-perel-technology-our-ability-cope-caroline-kealey/.

Korn Ferry. *The Nomad Economy.* n.d. https://www.kornferry.com/content/dam/kornferry/docs/article-migration/Briefings38_Nomad-Economy.pdf.

Kornfield, Jack. "Finding the Middle Way." Jack Kornfield Official Site. https://jackkornfield.com/finding-the-middle-way/.

Levitt, Jacob S., Constantinos G. V. Coutifaris, Paul I. Green Jr., and Sigal G. Barsade. "Timing Is Everything: An Imprinting Framework for the Implications of Leader Emotional Expressions for Team Member Social Worth and Performance." *Organization Science* 36, no. 1 (2024). https://doi.org/10.1287/orsc.2023.1739.

Loehnen, Elise. "Loving Mid-Life." *Pulling the Thread* (Substack), August 22, 2024. https://eliseloehnen.substack. com/p/loving-mid-life.

Loehnen, Elise. "Tapping into Creative Potential." *Pulling the Thread* (Substack), February 13, 2023. https://eliseloehnen. substack.com/p/tapping-into-creative-potential.

Madison, Caleb. "What Does It Feel Like to 'Be Seen'?" *The Atlantic*, December 17, 2021. https:// www.theatlantic.com/newsletters/archive/2021/12/ that-feeling-when-you-feel-seen/621050/.

Marcia, James E. "Development and Validation of Ego-Identity Status." *Journal of Personality and Social Psychology* 3, no. 5 (1966): 551–558. https://doi.org/10.1037/ h0023281

Maslow, Abraham H. *The Farther Reaches of Human Nature.* New York: Viking Press, 1971.

Osipow, Samuel H. "Career Development Models: A Brief Overview of Relevant Theory." *Journal of Career Development* 16, no. 1 (1989): 17–24. https://doi. org/10.1177/089484538901600103.

Oxford University Press. "Career." *Oxford English Dictionary Online.* https://www.oed.com.

Palmer, Parker J. *Let Your Life Speak: Listening for the Voice of Vocation.* San Francisco: Jossey-Bass, 2000.

Parsons, Frank. *Choosing a Vocation.* Boston: Houghton Mifflin, 1909.

Paxton, Shelley. *Soulbbatical: A Corporate Rebel's Guide to Finding Your Best Life.* New York: Tiller Press, 2020.

Perel, Esther. Quote referenced in: Kealey, Caroline. *LinkedIn*, October 3, 2023.

Piechowski, Michael M. "How Do Highly Gifted Adults Show Up?" *Positive Disintegration Newsletter* (Substack), May 1999. https://open.substack.com/pub/deborahruf/p/how-do-highly-gifted-adults-show.

Piechowski, Michael M. "Positive Disintegration and Self-Actualization." Paper presented at the 12th Annual Hollingworth Conference for Highly Gifted, Manchester, NH, May 1999.

Pressfield, Steven. *The War of Art: Break Through the Blocks and Win Your Inner Creative Battles*. New York: Black Irish Entertainment, 2002.

Rogers, Carl R. *On Becoming a Person: A Therapist's View of Psychotherapy*. Boston: Houghton Mifflin, 1970.

Rosenberg, Marshall B., and Deepak Chopra. *Nonviolent Communication: A Language of Life – Life-Changing Tools for Healthy Relationships*. Encinitas, CA: PuddleDancer Press, 2015.

Ruf, Deborah. "How Do Highly Gifted Adults Show Up?" *Positive Disintegration*, Substack, September 20, 2023. https://deborahruf.substack.com/p/how-do-highly-gifted-adults-show.

Santos, Laurie. "Top 5: Finding Joy in Any Job." *The Happiness Lab with Dr. Laurie Santos*. Podcast audio, November 14, 2024. https://omny.fm/shows/the-happiness-lab-with-dr-laurie-santos/birthday.

Seemiller, Corey. "Generation Z: Making a Difference Their Way." TEDx Talk. http://www.coreyseemiller.com/.

Sex and the City. "An American Girl in Paris, Part Deux."
Season 6, Episode 20. Directed by Michael Patrick King.
Aired February 22, 2004, on HBO.

Silverman, Linda K. *Giftedness in Adults Rating Scale.*
Denver, CO: Gifted Development Center, 2005.

Stanford Center on Longevity. *New Map of Life: Short Report
2.* Stanford University, April 2022. https://longevity.stanford.
edu/wp-content/uploads/2022/04/Short-Report-2.pdf.

Steinberg, Laurence D. *Age of Opportunity: Lessons from the
New Science of Adolescence.* New York: Houghton Mifflin
Harcourt, 2014.

Sturges, Jane, Michael Clinton, Neil Conway, and Alexandra
Budjanovcanin. "I Know Where I'm Going: Sensemaking and
the Emergence of Calling." *Journal of Vocational Behavior* 114
(2019): 103316. https://doi.org/10.1016/j.jvb.2019.02.002.

Super, Donald E. "A Life-Span, Life-Space Approach to
Career Development." *Journal of Vocational Behavior* 16
(1980): 282–298. https://doi.org/10.1016/0001-8791(80)90056-1.

Terkel, Studs. *Working: People Talk About What They Do All
Day and How They Feel About What They Do.* New York: New
Press, 1972.

Walton, Gregory M., and Shannon T. Brady. "Improving
Student Success Through Social Belonging." *Stanford News,*
May 25, 2023. https://news.stanford.edu/stories/2023/05/
improving-student-success-social-belonging.

Walton, Gregory M., and Shannon T. Brady. "The Many
Questions of Belonging." In *Handbook of Competence and
Motivation: Theory and Application,* 2nd ed., edited by
Andrew Elliot, Carol Dweck, and David Yeager, 272–293. New
York: Guilford Press, 2017.

Winsor, John, and Jin H. Paik. *Open Talent: Leveraging the Global Workforce to Solve Your Biggest Challenges*. New York: Harvard Business Review Press, 2024.

Whyte, David. *On Belonging & Coming Home*. Many Rivers & Seven Arrows. YouTube video, 2:02. Published 2009. https://www.youtube.com/watch?v=P92kymp1fxY.

Wrzesniewski, Amy, Jane E. Dutton, and Gelaye Debebe. "Interpersonal Sensemaking and the Meaning of Work." *Research in Organizational Behavior* 25 (2003): 93–135. https://doi.org/10.1016/S0191-3085(03)25003-6.

Yeung, King-To, and John Levi Martin. "The Looking Glass Self: An Empirical Test and Elaboration." *Social Forces* 81, no. 3 (2003): 843–879. https://doi.org/10.1353/sof.2003.0038.

Acknowledgements

Every book has its own way of coming into the world. My first book, *More Than My Title*, flowed out of me in that divine way authors dream about: it went from draft to published in just six months. But *Seen Known Valued*? It arrived through an entirely different process, one that tested my stamina and demanded deep persistence over three years. It came as a wild jungle of research, insights, and fragmented ideas over the course of two pregnancies. I nearly gave up multiple times. But determination is a weird drug, and now it's here! Truly, deeply, madly thank you to a cadre of critical supporters.

Many of the core ideas in this book were written when I was awake at 2 a.m., unable to sleep. I typed long notes on my smartphone while in bed, capturing fleeting thoughts, not yet knowing where they belonged. Later, with a newborn son cocooned in my lap, I typed one-handed, finally finding space to write. I ended up with an 80,000-word draft full of ideas, but my brain couldn't detangle it. Enter ChatGPT, which I openly credit as a key tool in helping me see my own thoughts. It helped uncover themes that shaped the key arguments.

Behind the scenes was a team of champions, each of whom mattered in bringing this book to life. I SEE and VALUE every single one of you. THANK YOU for providing mental clarity, emotional grounding, and endless hours of processing out loud.

The Book Team

I had two incredible developmental editors. Anne Janzer was my first book whisperer. She talked me off a major cliff when I had a wild idea at the eleventh hour. Her calm presence made all the difference. And then Melissa Killian swept in with laser focus and an eye for finding the core ideas that legitimately snapped everything into sharper focus. The book is tight and smooth because of them.

I used 99Designs and Fiverr, two incredible marketplaces for freelance creatives, for sourcing the perfect book cover and interior layout. I'm so glad these platforms exist.

I'm grateful to the incredible experts who helped anchor this book in broader, meaningful conversations: Dr. Joi Lin, Dr. Corey Seemiller, and Julie Winkle Giulioni generously shared their brilliance and contributed ideas that helped elevate this work.

Friends and Family

How is anything possible without a true partner who sees the real you? Brad Bickerton, the fearless, not-so-secretly incredible, JD/MBA/hybrid love of my life (all the heart emojis here). I'm not sure what we'll talk about anymore since we've been gabbing about this book endlessly on every stroller walk, car trip, chairlift ride, date night, and most nights in bed. He probably logged nearly as many thinking hours on this project as I did.

Our first nanny, Alisha, gave me the gift of sacred alone time and always apologized for interrupting, even when she didn't need to. Bev and Phil Freedman reminded me to practice self-compassion and self-care throughout the process, sending mindfulness tools when I felt depleted, and showing me what family belonging feels like.

Tara Gilboa has been my sister goddess and persistent book cheerleader. She's believed in my research since book one and hasn't lost steam. Julie Penner always picked up the phone to dish about our writing journeys and offer encouragement. Kate Bailey has been one of my rocks throughout. Brenna Vaughn, my ultimate role model of hybridity, has been my longest unwavering supporter. And, Liz Iraki and Kenzie Crow lifted my spirits when I wasn't sure what I was doing and the book cover design felt like an impossible task.

Book Champions

People from around the world gave feedback, joined focus groups, jumped on Zoom calls, and shared personal stories to shape this book. A special shoutout to those whose stories became central to its message: Nicholas

Whitaker, Sue McGurkin, Shelley Paxton, Bethany Crystal, and Yael Gavish. Their ideas and life paths had a profound influence on this work. They are truly redefining the future of work.

Special thanks to Kim Ribich (Career Clarity Specialist) and Kim Bilawchuk (The Career Inspirationalist), two phenomenal career coaches and former clients who are powerful forces in this movement.

Huge gratitude to my interviewees and focus group participants: Ella Hazard, Harris Rollinger, Taylor Harrington, Tracy Borreson, Vici Koster-Lenhardt, Amanda Gaube, Onyi Okechukwu, Anna Muir, Roger Malina, Bruce Wilhelm, SJ Kindsvatter, Kate Rodgers, Scott Phares, Melissa Rome, Radhika Rao, Tom Thorpe, Bob Rosen, Sara Steed, Lindsay Nason, Nora Welch, Stephanie Schmitz, Michelle Scheibner, Ashima Chopra, Elana Merzin, Risa Zenno, Helene Maltzman, Kasper Daems, Evi Kathrepti, Laetitia de Haas, and Emilia Montiglio (and others whose contributions I hold with deep gratitude).

Finally, thank you to those who offered encouragement from afar—through LinkedIn, emails, and unexpected moments of connection: Jerry Colonna, April Rinne, Rich Feller, Andrew Hyde, Marci Alboher, Natalie Lampert, Vijay Pendakur, Zach Mercurio, Jasna Klemenc Puntar, Bree Groff, Dustin Liu, Oana Leonte, John Carter, Christina Doepper, Becky Baker, Chris Hanff, Dana Grinnell, CJ Juleff, and Kate Holgate. You made me realize I am part of something greater than I knew.

About the Author

Dr. Sarabeth Berk Bickerton is a trailblazer in the future of work and the leading expert on hybrid professional identity and career belonging. A TEDx speaker and author of More Than My Title, her groundbreaking research redefines how professionals are seen, known, and valued beyond traditional job titles. Sarabeth calls herself a Creative Disruptor, blending her identities as an artist, researcher, educator, and designer. Her journey began in the midst of a professional identity crisis that revealed her most valuable insight: true power lies not in choosing one title, but in integrating multiple identities. That epiphany became the foundation of her work. Today, she empowers jacks-of-all-trades and multipotentialites to articulate their unique value and find deeper belonging in their work through one-of-a-kind identity-based career strategies and personal branding.